STRESS
FoodBook

- **The Stress Relief Diet**
  — A Six Meal-a-Day Emergency Plan

- **The Stress Prevention Diet**
  — A Three Meal-a-Day Lifetime Plan

- **209 Stress-Reducing Recipes**

- **Stress Management**
  — Without Weight Gain

- **Everyday Foods Nutritionists
  Use to Reduce Stress**

THE NATURAL WAY TO FIGHT STRESS . . .   THE **RIGHT** FOODS

THE STRESS FoodBook

Margaret C. Dean, M.S., R.D.
illustrations by Loel Barr

A ACROPOLIS BOOKS LTD.
Washington, D.C.

ACROPOLIS BOOKS LTD.
Colortone Building, 2400 17th St., N.W.
Washington, D.C. 20009

Printed in the United States of America by
COLORTONE PRESS Creative Graphics, Inc.
Washington, D.C. 20009

Library of Congress Cataloging in Publication Data

Dean, Margaret C., 1919-
    The stress foodbook.

    Includes index.
    1. Stress (Psychology)—Prevention.   2. Stress
(Physiology)—Prevention.   3. Diet therapy—Recipes.
I. Title.
BF575.S75D35   613.2'6   81-20584
ISBN 0-87491-295-4 (pbk.)   AACR2

Dedication

*T*his Book Is Lovingly Dedicated
To The Memory Of My Brother
William Marvin 'Bill' Carter

With heavy business responsibilities, my brother learned how to manage situations that would overcome the average individual. His energy, enthusiasm, love for others and dynamic qualities of leadership enabled him to deal with heavy stresses and turn them into successes. His was an exemplary life. Helping others seemed to be his life's goal. His last contribution to mankind was assisting another person who needed help.

Because of his ability to free himself from stress, he was able to devote more of his energies to productive work. One of the ways that he relaxed was playing hymns or other music on a small organ which he had placed in his office. He accomplished more in his short life span than most persons do in a long number of years.

During his life he was forever helping others. It is appropriate, therefore, that a scholarship has been established in his name at Virginia Polytechnic Institute and State University, his Alma Mater. In this way a young student in the Forestry and Wildlife College will be helped to get a college education.

Acknowledgments

*O*ur society is filled with stress-causing factors and they appear to be on the increase. But taking time out to smell the roses has given me time to make friends who know how to exert positive energy while maintaining a sensitivity to human needs around them. Such a friend is Dr. Mildred Tate, a teacher, counselor and a professional with tremendous leadership qualities. I thank her for her teachings and guidance.

I thank my dear friend, the late Dr. Virginia McMasters of the University of California who made possible many opportunities for testing and demonstrating new ideas. She was a positive, dynamic force in my life and in every life that her life touched.

The author gratefully acknowledges the assistance of Kate Bandos and her husband, Doug for their suggestions and assistance with my books.

Thanks go to Sandy Trupp for her encouragement; Kathleen Hughes and Laurie Tag for their cheerful criticisms, suggestions and patience; Debra Salem for serving as one of the editors; friends and colleagues who have been encouraging and helpful and to the patients who have been generous with information during the nutrition assessment studies.

Special appreciation to nutritionists and dietitions all over the United States and abroad who have responded to my questionnaire. Thank you to the teams of physicians, psychiatrists, psychologists, pharmacists, social workers and nurses who have included me as a team member and taught me the basics of this book.

To my daughter, Marge, many thanks for daily encouragement and for reviewing and making suggestions on the manuscript.

And finally, to my dear husband whom I can never thank enough for his tremendous help and of whom I am very proud.

Contents

Introduction

Stress in Everyday Life

*E*veryone lives under almost constant stress from childhood through old age. But what is stress? Stress may be defined as any change — for better or worse — that is accompanied by some discomfort, either mental or physical. It can affect the functions of both the mind and the body.

Of course, some tensions and challenges are good for us. Life without change and the richness of personal experience is dull indeed. In fact, our bodies are constructed to react to most stresses without suffering serious damage.

However, when your body is exposed to too much stress, or stress that lasts too long, it can react negatively. This reaction can be emotional, behavioral, or psychological. It is the psychological response that can actually induce backaches, migraine headaches, gastrointestinal ulcers, allergies, asthma, high blood pressure, even heart disease and cancer.

As a dietitian and nutritionist, I have helped to bandage the physical, mental, and emotional wounds of people caught up in calamity. I know from first-hand experience how the right foods help relieve stress and begin the process of healing. Unfortunately, most people don't know what these foods are, how much, or when to eat them.

With the assistance of the health care team of doctors, dentists, nurses, fellow dietitians and nutritionists, social workers, pharmacists, psychologists, psychiatrists, and health educators, I have spent years researching stress, stress prevention, and treatment in medical facilities and rehabilitation centers.

Obesity, the number one health problem in our country, can be easily related to stress, as can smoking, drug, and alcohol abuse. Studies show that, under stress, we immediately crave food. It is equated in our minds with security and satisfaction. And most of us eat sweet foods and snacks too heavy in fats, sugars, and salt.

Although overeating is an obvious culprit in causing obesity, our lifestyle must be considered as well. For many, sedentary work and living habits should determine the amount of food eating. And our individual likes and dislikes must be taken into account when we plan any dietary changes.

Your lifestyle may call for a diet pattern that you can live with the rest of your life. The Stress Diet is just that regimen. You will find it is a six-meal plan for preventing disease and also for treating the effects of stress. The pattern calls for breakfast, midmorning snack, lunch, midafternoon snack, dinner, and bedtime snack. You will find this a pattern that will adjust your body to having a manageable quantity of food in the stomach at all times, never overloading the gastrointestinal system. This prevents food overload and keeps your inner body more tranquil, stable, and safe from digestive extremes. Milk serves as the basic food since it is comparatively high in nutrition.

This book presents a complete and comprehensive discussion of stress with hundreds of menus and recipes to show how foods bring about the best nutritional status for the body. It concludes with the moderation, or three-meal, diet which can become a six-meal plan if desired.

You might consider it strange that a plan for reducing stress includes recipes calling for sugar, salt and unsaturated fats — considered key culprits in producing stress — however, in moderation, these will not cause added stress to your body. In fact, you need moderate amounts of these items to meet the chemical requirements of the body under stress.

Another seeming irony is the recommendation of tea in this stress relief program. We emphasize tea for two reasons. First, for most people tea serves as a catalyst for relaxation. Hot tea, sipped slowly within the few minutes needed for a break, can change your attitude toward yourself, your work, and your family. Second, the flavor of tea blends with the high nutritional fruit juices which are important in this approach to stress control. Although tea does contain a little caffeine, it contains far less than coffee. And tea's beneficial effects far outweigh any negative effects of the caffeine it contains.

I hope that you will find the Stress Foodbook helpful in managing the stress you face in your daily life. Nothing will magically make problems disappear, but allowing your body to do its best to combat the damage stress can cause will give you a healthier, more serene lifestyle.

Margaret C. Dean, M.S., R.D.

Chapter One

Stress and the Toll it Takes on Your Body

A Working Definition of Stress

Stress is considered by many experts to be the most serious health problem of our time. Stress is studied by medical doctors, health educators, psychiatrists, pharmacists, social workers, and nutritionists. It increases blood pressure, heartbeat, hormone and acid production, bladder pressure, and red cell counts. Stress quickens breathing, dilates pupils, contracts intestinal muscle and blood vessels and decreases rates of blood clotting. Stress can cause blindness, diabetes, cirrhosis of the liver, deafness, paralysis, arthritis, migraine headaches, asthma, backache, and gastrointestinal ulcers. It is also being studied as a factor in the development of cancer. Stress is a slowly ticking time bomb, just waiting to detonate. It kills thousands of people every year.

What, exactly, is stress, where does it come from, and how has it assumed such an important role in our daily lives?

In simple terms, a stress may be defined as any change, for better or worse, in your external environment that is reflected in wear-and-tear on your body. Your internal environment — the workings of your inner self, your spirit, and the actual chemical composition of your body — is affected by the whole outside world. How well you adapt to life depends largely upon how well your internal environment tolerates the external environment.

Stress doesn't have to be damaging. Some stresses may be positive and provide the underlying motivation for achievements. For instance, stress is responsible for a marathon runner's burst of competitive spirit, an actor's performance before a sell-out crowd, and an employee's desire for promotion. These positive stresses contribute toward change, progress, and the richness of varied personal experiences in our lives. Our bodies are designed to respond to challenges and dangers, both physical and mental. If the human body could not handle stress, it certainly would not have evolved as far as it has.

It is true that modern technology has removed or simplified many of the tasks that were hardships for our forebearers. Travel, now, is effortless rather than life threatening; modern medicine saves the lives of people who would have died. We have come very far, indeed, in our application of new technology for the development of sophisticated systems, but we have not learned how to live stress-free lives.

Today, stress is more complicated. In addition to the stress of personal tragedies and triumphs — are worries about society as a whole. We feel stress not only within our family units but within the entire nation. Thanks to the mixed blessings of technology, we can learn about an earthquake in Japan and daily changes within the smallest country in the world instantly. And we react just as swiftly. The troubles of the whole world, in short, are our troubles.

Our enormously sophisticated society involves us more and more frequently in mental tasks and less and less in physical labor. We live at a faster pace and are highly dependent upon other people and machines. We aspire to higher status, yet we are afraid of losing what security we do have.

In the midst of such a rapidly changing environment, we dash out in the morning on an empty stomach and try to stave off hunger by snatching a quick bite at a drive-in.

In trying to deal with new pressures, we use more and more processed foods manufactured by new technologies. These new technologies have changed the food supply itself both by making more foods available more often and by creating new foods.

Wheat and corn are turned into foods such as sugar coated puffed cereals. With the aid of a little food-coloring, added fats, sugar and salt, technology has given us tasty foods which have little nutritive value and may cause health problems in children. Hamburgers produced by added varied amounts of "fillers" — the most common being soybeans — do not contain all of the amino acides necessary for proper growth and tissue development in children.

Technology has created, along with its new foods made out of artificial sweeteners and coloring, a strong skepticism in the minds of many Americans about just exactly what it is they *are* eating: is it healthful, is it harmful, is it natural?

The nutritional changes in the foods we eat,

in and of themselves, would be stressful enough to our bodies, but there are many other specific stresses that are a part of our lives and with which we must manage.

Let's take a look at some of them. All are affected directly or indirectly by our internal and/or external environments.

The Causes of Stress

Any number of events in our lives create stress. The death of a spouse, a divorce, or separation are considered highly stressful situations; getting married, fired, pregnant or retiring are considered moderately stressful; a large mortgage, children who are leaving home, moving to a new home, trouble with in-laws, a change in school, a vacation, and the Christmas holidays are considered somewhat stressful. Any dramatic change, good or bad, will produce stress on your body.

How much stress is too much? How does stress relate to the normal functioning of your body? Does environment play a part and does it affect our food habits? Does a particular kind of stress bring on disease or is stress a significant factor only when linked with other factors such as diet, smoking habits, and high blood pressure?

We don't know the answers to all of these questions. We can conclude that stress affects each person in a different way. The specific cause of stress is not as important as our reactions to the stress.

Whatever the cause for stress, it usually affects us in stages and we respond accordingly.

Stress and Your Body

Your body operates on an alarm system that is activated regardless of the source of stress: Stage 1 —alarm; Stage 2 — resistance, and Stage 3 — exhaustion. In the alarm stage, your body recognized that it is under stress and prepares either to fight back or flee from the source. Part of this "batten-down-the-hatches" response is a slowed digestion of foods in the stomach; energy is taken from the digestive system and directed into the muscle and nervous systems in preparation for physical activity.

In the resistance stage, your body tries to undo any damage done by the stress response once the "danger" is perceived to be past. If the stress remains, however, your body cannot repair itself and must remain on the alert.

A state of continued alert plunges the body into exhaustion, the third stage of the alarm system. Prolonged exhaustion can cause one of the stress-related diseases mentioned earlier.

Stress will manifest itself in one of three ways: in emotional, behavioral or psychological response. Fear, rage, and tantrums are emotional responses; changes in overt behavior patterns are considered behavioral responses; and psychological responses will trigger head-aches, backaches, ulcers, allergies, and heart disease.

Emotional responses will cause your heart to palpitate, your muscles to tremble visibly; your digestive organs to cease functioning and your blood to rush irregularly throughout your body. Emotional responses to stress can cause psychological responses. How can this happen?

The most basic stress begins in the very center of the brain, the hypothalmus. This small bundle of body cells regulates growth, sex, and reproduction. These body functions are related also to the functions of protein in the diet. Protein is the food nutrient responsible for promoting growth and maintaining life, as well as building and repairing body tissues.

In directing the basic physiological changes involved in stress, the hypothalmus acts in two ways: it controls the automatic nervous system which regulates the involuntary activities of the body's functions, and it activates the pituitary gland which orders the release of chemical messengers, or hormones, that produce powerful signals the body must heed. Together, the hypothalmus and the pituitary gland alter the functioning of almost every part of the body. Stress can unbalance these functions and throw the body out of control. (See chart on page 17).

Your body muscles become tense at the command of the autonomic nervous system. Faster breathing may result. Your heart rate increases and blood vessels constrict, raising the blood pressure and almost completely closing the blood vessels that lie just beneath the skin. Your stomach and intestines temporarily halt digestion, while the muscles controlling the intestines and bladder loosen. In other parts of the body the autonomic nervous system affects other changes; respiration increases, saliva secretion decreases and the pupils of your eyes may dilate.

The autonomic nerves stimulate the adrenal glands to release hormones. Hormones, in turn, affect the circulation of the blood, reinforcing the autonomic nervous system's action in elevating heartbeat and blood pressure. The adrenals increase the amount of fat in the blood since body fat is broken down, and the liver is stimulated to produce more sugar.

The pituitary gland also reacts to commands of the hypothalmus. It secretes two hormones that play a major role in the basic stress response. The tyrotropic hormone stimulates the thyroid which increases the rate at which the body produces energy. Another hormone from the pituitary gland reinforces the signal sent to the adrenal glands through the autonomic nervous system.

If the body must use its energy to response to stress, then it cannot use the same energy to perform normal bodily functions. Doctors consider fatigue a warning signal that the body is under too much stress.

Effects of Stress on the Body

The brain exercises complete control over every system of the body — circulation, respiration, digestion absorption.

There are a number of readily identifiable responses to stress, as we have said. Emotional responses, such as anger, can result in psychological responses with physical consequences. Ulcers (holes in the lining of the gastrointestinal tract), colitis (infection of the colon), spastic colon (expansion and restriction of the colon), and hiatal hernia are all results of the body's attempts to deal with an unacceptable environment — results that take their toll on your stomach.

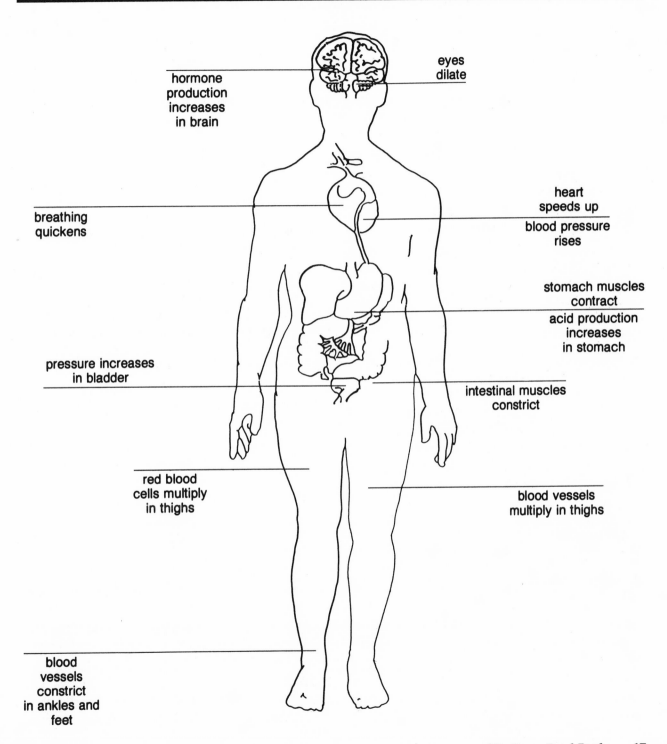

eyes
dilate

hormone
production
increases
in brain

heart
speeds up

blood pressure
rises

breathing
quickens

stomach muscles
contract

acid production
increases
in stomach

pressure increases
in bladder

intestinal muscles
constrict

red blood
cells multiply
in thighs

blood vessels
multiply in thighs

blood
vessels
constrict
in ankles and
feet

Common Escapes from Stress

Since stress does not come from germs or viruses, many of us may not realize that stress can lead to chronic physical ailments such as those we have listed, as well as to drug abuse, alcoholism, family breakdown, suicide, or loss of job. Some of these problems are direct attempts to escape from stress and several of them are particularly destructive to your health.

Alcoholism

Research shows that most alcoholics replace food with alcohol. They begin with small amounts. As their tolerance increases, alcoholics crave larger and larger quantities of alcohol and smaller and smaller quantities of food. It is easy for a cocktail drinker to consume 1200 to 1500 calories a day, enough to satisfy the caloric need of someone with a sedentary lifestyle.

Most alcoholics suffer from malnutrition brought on by a derangement of the appetite mechanism found in the brain. Often the sight or smell of food becomes repulsive. But you can protect yourself from alcoholism. Studies show that a young child whose body composition has grown accustomed to white sugar, white flour products, white rice, and poor nutrition is more susceptible to alcoholism than is a child who has formed good eating habits early in life. Any person who eats a diet adequate to meet his body's needs will not have the appetite for consuming much alcohol.

Smoking

Many people smoke to relieve stress. Recent studies of smokers in Los Angeles show smoking is related to depression caused by a negative self image among smokers.

Smokers have been shown to eat more and weigh less, 5.5 pounds on average, than nonsmokers, yet they consume approximately 150 calories more a day. Increased utilization of calories due to adrenalin release, increased bowel motility, decreased food absorption (foods may be consumed, digested but not absorbed into the blood stream in the small intestine), or increased nervousness may all account for this discrepancy. Although, on the surface, lower weight might seem to be advantageous for smokers, these other physical affects are not healthy.

Overeating

Food, any food, can represent security, love, appreciation, and recognition. Food can begin or end wars, bring people together in jobs or destroy empires. Food can make a criminal out of a hungry child. In some cultures, food supply may be considered a basis for judging the wealth of an individual, but studies show that wealth alone is not enough to ensure that you are receiving enough of the right foods. In fact,

consuming great quantities of food of any type can contribute to overeating problems.

Early man had to search for his food on a daily basis. His diet was simple and natural, without preservatives or additives. It was vegetarian with grains and plants or high-protein with meat, depending upon the time in history and location in the world. Primarily grain eating or primarily meat eating people ate a combination of meats, vegetables, fruits and breads, when they were available. The well rounded diet was known for many years prior to today.

Man in the past adapted to his environment. He demonstrated great ability to adjust and thrive under a variety of stressful situations. Modern man is in danger of relieving stress with excessive use of foods that are already affecting the body's defense mechanism and causing increases in certain diseases. We also select, according to studies, high fat (usually saturated fats), high sugar, high salt and, low fiber foods, and alcohol. We prefer them to an adequate diet based on a variety of foods, whole grain cereals, breads, fresh fruits, and vegetables.

The excessive intake of sugars, fats, and salt has created an alarming number of obese Americans. A recent study of obesity shows that six hundred obese women were assessed nutrionally and one third were nutritionally deficient. Obesity is definitely not an indicator of good nutrition or health.

The foods we crave under stress are usually just the opposite of what our body needs. If you are prone to excessive alcohol use or to diabetes, you desire sugar above all other foods. If you have a tendency toward heart disease, you crave salt. If you are bored or restless, you usually crave foods high in carbohydrates and fats; they are very satisfying and make you feel full. Potato chips or small, crunchy items that keep you busy are the most popular. Every day nutritionists see people with poor eating habits which are the results of stress. The challenge is to improve those habits and improve health at the same time.

As in all things, moderation in eating is recommended. This is especially important during stressful periods when only the amount of food necessary to meet your body's needs should be consumed.

When consumed in excess, many foods — particularly sugar, salt, and saturated fats — are unhealthy. But *in moderation* these foods do not add stress to the body. And their consumption, in limited quantities such as found in the recipes in this book, helps meet the changing nutritional needs of the body under stress.

Most of us are unable to limit ourselves to food choices that are good for us unless we have practiced a routine of thinking about our health maintenance. The six-meal stress relief and prevention diets in Chapters Two and Three can help you learn to choose more wisely from what is available in our abundant food supply systems and develop eating patterns appropriate to your individual needs.

Everything in life needs to be kept in balance. Life is your precious gift; live it healthfully — that will be the greatest of all benefits from good nutrition.

A Personal Stress-Reducing Inventory

Take an inventory of yourself; make it a habit. Keep the results to yourself, with a determination to work on each point you wish to improve.

1. Moderation is the key word. All activities of life should be kept in moderation.
2. Follow the stress relief diet; return to the basics, and follow a routine.
3. Learn to breathe correctly. The brain requires 16 times more oxygen than any other organ of the body. Correct breathing will stimulate circulation; it invigorates the whole body, aids digestion, induces sleep, soothes the nerves, and promotes peace of mind. Careful breathing helps us relax under most any kind of stress or tension.
4. Lower your own metabolism by: sitting quietly, closing your eyes, and relaxing each area of your body by breathing through your nose and thinking about relaxing each area of the body.
5. Exercise each day. Walking is the best exercise. Select your distance and make it routine.

Moderation in all things, especially your diet.

Your diet becomes you — as will the thoughts you think.

Chapter Two

The Stress Relief Diet: A Six-Meal-a-Day Plan

*T*his diet plan is one you can follow during periods of heavy stress. It is a six-meal approach that uses frequent but moderate sized meals to fuel your body without overtaxing it.

All the foods are simple and easy to digest. The plan includes a great deal of milk, the most nearly perfect food which supplies the protein, minerals, and vitamins needed to keep the tissues of the digestive tract in good repair and well-coated.

The Milk Solution

Americans are spending nearly half a billion dollars annually on 575 different commercial preparations for digestive relief. Taken in excess, these drugs can cause serious side effects increasing stress in an already stress laden body.

The simplest, best tasting, and most effective concoction you can take when feeling upset is a glass of milk. If you have a stomach problem because you ate too hurriedly, or you were too worried, or you ate too much or too little, sip some milk. However, if the pain persists, or you don't know it's origin, see a doctor as well. In the meantime, try some milk, for it can make the gastrointestinal tract feel so much better. It is easily digested unless you have a lactose problem and lack the enzyme that breaks down lactose, the milk sugar.

Whole milk soothes because it is a combination of protein, carbohydrate, and fat suitable for a baby's delicate system or an older person's lowered metabolism. The milk's protein heals the body cells being destroyed. The milk's fat coats any damaged area to prevent irritation caused by foods passing through the digestive tract.

The human body daily undergoes a wearing away of body cells; protein in the diet, with the help of vitamins, builds back the lost cells. Under stress, the body tissues are subjected to an above-normal rate of loss.

If unrelieved, this process can bring on chronic illness. A very good example is the constant elevation of glucose (sugar) in the blood causing the pancreas to work at a high rate to bring the glucose levels back to normal. An overworked pancreas finally develops pancreatitis due to stress overload. The elevation of glucose may have been caused by heavy intake of sugars or starches — including alcohol — or just too much indulgence of all foods. In this case, treatment, rather than prevention, is necessary.

Your Stress Threshold

Tensions and pressures build when you are racing against time, failing to listen to the rhythm of your body. Each of us is a different biological being operating at a different pace. It is wise to know your pace and stay within it. When you feel that you are constantly pressured, you are then living under stress. The point where pace changes to pressure is your "stress threshold."

Become aware of your stress threshold and avoid prolonged stress, for it will unbalance your diet. When under stress, reduce your food intake. Any diet required to reduce cholesterol involves a reduction in total calories, substitution of polyunsaturated fat for saturated fat and a lessening of emotional tension.

If you crave food under stress, however, there are some simple, easy to eat snack and small meals:

- Glass of milk (whole or nonfat) with toast cubes.
- Hot soups such as cream of chicken, chicken rice, cream of cheddar cheese, cream of carrot, cream of mushroom and peanut.
- Hot tea with lemon.
- Hot baked potato with vegetable fat (except coconut oil)
- Iced nonfat milk
- Fruit juices or lemonade
- Gelatin cubes with fruit sauce topping
- Fruit punch or fruit ice

If you can tolerate a full meal, here are a few suggestions:

- Meal should be very low in fat or fat-free
- Prolonged stress requires a special controlled fat diet.
- Soft foods ease food's passage along the gastrointestinal tract.
- Milk will coat the lining of the digestive tract and prevent irritation

Restricting all foods for a short period appears to be better for your body when it is under extremely heavy stress. Restricting all foods, however, for more than one day, can be life-destructing and create stress or add to already existing stress. Fast for more than a day only with the advice of a physician.

The Stress Relief Diet

Foods that decrease the work load of the digestive processes and that can be used by the body without stimulation of the heart, nerve, or muscle functions, can be considered "tranquil" in nature. These are desirable foods when you are under stress.

I have developed a six-meal-a-day plan that can help your body cope with highly stressful situations.

Once your body becomes adjusted to the six-meal diet, you'll be surprised at how much better you feel. Your body will not be overworked trying to digest too many high fat, salty, or sweet foods. You will not feel full from eating big meals.

A routine diet pattern containing about the same amount of food for each of six meals is especially needed by sedentary people for whom stress can be more upsetting than to those who are physically active.

Note: This diet should not be confused with the hospital bland diet: the "anti-stress" diet is a disease *prevention* diet, while the hospital diet is for *treatment* of disease. If you are on a bland diet already, you will want to remain on it, or if you have an ulcer — or think you do — see your doctor.

Seven days of menus for the six-meal stress relief diet, including recipes, follow. It can become your lifetime eating pattern.

*Calorie value for each day approximately 1500-1600.

Day One

BREAKFAST
½ cup fruit juice (preferably orange)
½ cup hot cereal
½ cup low-fat milk

MIDMORNING
½ cup nonfat milk
toast cubes

LUNCH
½ cup vegetable broth with crackers
baked potato in jacket*
1 teaspoon vegetable fat
½ cup sliced peaches

MIDAFTERNOON
½ cup nonfat milk
gelatin cubes with topping

DINNER
baked chicken a la pineapple* over steamed rice
½ cup nonfat milk
lemon sherbet* or cranberry sherbet*

BEDTIME
1 cup warm or cold nonfat milk
cubed pears

*Recipes follow

Note:
*Nonfat milk may be skim liquid, reconstituted dry nonfat milk or buttermilk.

Day Two

BREAKFAST
½ cup applesauce
½ cup hot cereal
1 teaspoon vegetable fat
½ cup nonfat milk

MIDMORNING
½ cup orange juice
1 slice toast
1 teaspoon vegetable fat

LUNCH
1 cup quick potato soup* with crackers or luxery leek
    potato soup*
fish fillet in a skillet*
½ cup aspasagus spears
pear half
½ cup nonfat milk

MIDAFTERNOON
special hot spiced tea with lemon*
2 graham crackers

DINNER
½ cup tomato consomme* or tomato madrilene
½ cup macaroni-and-cheese bake*
½ cup steamed spinach
1 teaspoon vegetable fat
½ cup sliced peaches

BEDTIME
1 cup cheese soup* or
1 cup mushroom soup*

*Recipes follow

Day Three

BREAKFAST
½ cup orange juice
1 soft scrambled egg Supreme*
1 blueberry coffee cake* slice
1 teaspoon vegetable fat
½ cup nonfat milk

MIDMORNING
1 slice toast
coffee with cream and sugar

LUNCH
beef broth oriental* with crackers
mashed potato
½ cup sliced beets
½ cup nonfat milk

MIDAFTERNOON
½ cup mixed fruit cup*

DINNER
broiled lamb chop
½ cup green beans
tomato-and-lettuce salad*
1 teaspoon French dressing, Special*
1 slice whole-wheat bread
1 teaspoon vegetable fat
lemonade or cranberry punch*

BEDTIME
½ cup milk
toast cubes

*Recipes follow

Day Four

BREAKFAST
½ grapefruit
½ cup cream of wheat
1 teaspoon vegetable fat
½ cup nonfat milk
1 soft-cooked egg
1 slice whole grain bread

MIDMORNING
hot spiced tea with lemon* cream, and sugar

LUNCH
1 cup cream of watercress soup* with crackers
melted cheese over 1 slice mixed grain toast
vanilla ice cream
coffee with cream and sugar

MIDAFTERNOON
½ cup nonfat milk
½ cup orange sections

DINNER
baked meatloaf with herbs and tomato sauce*
stuffed baked potato-half creole*
½ cup chopped kale
½ cup mixed fruit
Island Fruit punch*

BEDTIME
1 slice toast
½ cup nonfat milk

*Recipes follow

Day Five

BREAKFAST
½ cup orange juice
½ cup cornflakes
½ cup nonfat milk
1 slice toast
1 tablespoon peanut butter (smooth)

MIDMORNING
plain cake donut
coffee with cream and sugar

LUNCH
1 cup vegetable soup* with crackers
tunafish salad or sweet-sour tune* on toast
1 slice whole grain toast
tomato slices
½ cup nonfat milk

MIDAFTERNOON
hot spiced tea with lemon*
lemon cookie

DINNER
1 slice baked chicken with lemon wedge
½ cup steamed rice and orange slices
½ cup steamed carrots and green peas
½ cup chopped lettuce and spinach
1 teaspoon creamy cucumber salad dressing*
½ cup nonfat milk

BEDTIME
1 cup creamy potato soup*

*Recipes follow

Day Six

BREAKFAST
½ cup orange juice
½ cup hot cereal
1 teaspoon vegetable fat
½ cup nonfat milk
1 slice raisin toast*

MIDMORNING
coffee with cream and sugar

LUNCH
cheese-topped stuffed tomato half*
orange and cottage cheese salad
lemon-lime gelatin cubes
½ cup nonfat milk

MIDAFTERNOON
½ cup clear broth

DINNER
1 cup cheese souffle*
½ cup tomato and cucumber slices
baking-powder biscuit*
½ cup nonfat milk
½ cup "Bill's Special" ambrosia*

BEDTIME
½ cup nonfat milk

Day Seven

BREAKFAST
1 medium baked apple with cinnamon*
cheese omelet (1 egg)
1 slice toast
1 teaspoon vegetable fat
coffee with cream and sugar

MIDMORNING
½ cup nonfat milk

LUNCH
1 slice roast turkey with sage or cornbread dressing*
½ cup broccoli
½ cup tossed salad*
1 teaspoon vegetable fat
½ cup orange and grapefruit slices
minted lemonade

MIDAFTERNOON
1 slice date–nut bread* with cream cheese
hot tea with lemon

DINNER
egg salad on toast*
stuffed peach half on lettuce
baked custard*
½ cup nonfat milk

BEDTIME
1 cup milk toast*

*Recipes follow

*Recipes follow

Recipes: Day One

Lemon Sherbet

½ cup lemon juice
1½ cups sugar
1 quart nonfat milk
lemon slices
mint leaves

Mix together the lemon juice and sugar. Add slowly to the milk, stirring constantly. Milk should never be added to lemon juice because of the danger of curdling. Place mixture in freezer tray or pan and freeze to a mushy consistency. Serve in sherbet dishes. Garnish each dish with lemon slice and mint leaf. Makes 6-8 one-half cup servings of 125 calories each.

Cranberry Sherbet

2 cups cranberries
1¼ cups water
½ cup sugar
1 teaspoon unflavored gelatin
½ cup cold water
juice of 1 lemon or 2 teaspoons lemon juice

Cook cranberries in 1¼ cups water until skins pop. Press through sieve. Add sugar and cook until sugar dissolves. Add gelatin softened in cold water; cool. Add lemon juice. Freeze in shallow pan or refrigerator tray 2 to 3 hours, stirring twice. Makes 6 one-half cup servings of 100 calories each.

Baked Potato in Jacket

1 baking potato

Wash and dry potato. Wrap in foil. Bake in oven at 375 degrees for an hour, or until done. Test the potato with fork. If foil can be easily pierced to potato's center, the potato is done.

Split foil and potato through. With thumb and forefinger, push potato open. Fill center with cottage cheese, french onion dip, sour cream, or vegetable fat, and a dash of salt. Makes one 100-calorie serving.

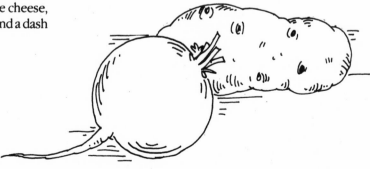

Chicken a la Pineapple

1 (3-pound size) broiler fryer, cut up
½ tablespoon sage
¼ teaspoon salt
1½ cups bread crumbs
2 teaspoons dried rosemary leaves
1 teaspoon ginger
½ cup finely-chopped celery
1 tablespoon orange peel
1 tablespoon vegetable fat, melted (except coconut oil)
¼ cup drained crushed pineapple
¼ cup orange juice
¼ cup pineapple juice
10 shallots, peeled
½ cup water

Remove skin from chicken. Rinse the chicken with cold water and drain. Dry inside and outside. Rub cavity of each chicken piece with sage and salt. Combine bread crumbs, rosemary, ginger, celery, orange peel, and fat in a bowl. Toss lightly. Place pieces of chicken in baking dish. Pour crushed pineapple, orange juice, and pineapple juice over the chicken. Add water and place chicken in oven. Bake at 375 degrees for about 1 hour or until chicken is tender. Makes 5-6 4-ounce servings of 145 calories each.

Quick Potato Soup

2 cups thinly sliced raw potatoes
½ cup finely chopped onion
1¼ cups boiling water
1½ cups nonfat milk
1 tablespoon vegetable fat (except coconut oil)
¼ teaspoon Worcestershire sauce
1 teaspoon salt
pepper

Add potatoes and onion to the boiling water. Cover and cook for 15 to 20 minutes or until potatoes are tender. Mash the potatoes slightly with a fork to thicken the soup a little, if desired. Add milk, fat, and seasonings. Heat. For a touch of color, garnish each serving with chopped parsley, grated cheese, croutons, diced crisp bacon or finely cut watercress or chives. Makes 4 one-cup servings of 50 calories each.

Special Consommé

1 tablespoon unflavored gelatin
2 cups well-seasoned soup stock or consommé
sliced lemon
minced parsley

Soften gelatin in ¼ cup stock. Heat remainder of stock and stir into gelatin. Chill. When set, beat lightly with a fork and serve in soup cups. Serve each with slice of lemon dipped in parsley. Makes 3-4 one-cup servings of 25 calories each.

Special Hot Spiced Tea

2 quarts water
½ cup loose orange pekoe tea or 8 tea bags
2 cup sugar
2 cups lemonade (frozen reconstituted)
2 cups orange juice (frozen reconstituted)
6 cloves
cinnamon

Heat water to just below boiling. Place in tea ball with loose tea or tea bags. Allow to steep. (Tea should be strong.) Remove tea ball or bags. Place back over heat. Add sugar and stir. Then add lemonade and orange juice. Heat to below boiling. Turn off heat. Add cloves and cinnamon. Tea may be stored in refrigerator and quantity reheated as needed. Keep tightly covered. Makes 24 one-cup servings of 75 calories each.

Fish Fillet in Skillet

1 pound fish fillets or steaks
3 tablespoons vegetable fat (except coconut oil)
1 chopped onion
3 tablespoons green pepper
2 tablespoons chopped parsley
2 medium tomatoes cut in pieces
½ cup water or tomato juice
½ teaspoon salt
½ teaspoon basil or oregano

If fish is frozen, thaw it to separate pieces. Heat oil in skillet. Add chopped onion, green pepper, and parsley; cook until soft. Add tomatoes, water or tomato juice, and seasoning; cook until tomatoes are soft. Add fish; cover and cook gently about 10 minutes or until fish is done. Makes 4 four-ounce servings of 150 calories each.

Luxury Leek Potato Soup

3 large potatoes, peeled and sliced thin
6 leeks, sliced thin
¼ cup chopped onion
2 tablespoons flour
2 cups nonfat milk
4 cups bouillon, heated (beef is best)
1 tablespoon minced parsley
1 tablespoon minced chervil or ½ teaspoon dry chervil

Cook potatoes until tender in small amount of water. Add leeks and onion. Make paste of flour and milk. Stir in potato mixture slowly. Add hot bouillon a little at a time, stirring. Simmer 8 to 10 minutes, stirring constantly. Add parsley and chervil. Serve with toasted rolls. Makes 4 one-cup servings of 125 calories each.

Cream of Cheddar Cheese Soup

½ cup finely chopped carrot

½ cup finely chopped onion

¼ cup finely chopped celery

2 tablespoons vegetable fat (except coconut oil)

¼ cup all-purpose flour

1 cup chicken broth (see page 45)

¼ teaspoon salt

2 cups milk

1½ cups cheddar cheese (6 ounces)

In covered saucepan, cook carrots, onion, and celery in vegetable fat over low heat until tender. Stir in flour. Add broth and salt. Cook and stir until thickened and bubbly. Stir in milk and cheese until cheese melts and soup is heated thoroughly. Do not boil. Makes 4-6 one-cup servings of 150 calories each.

Mushroom Soup, Creamed

2 cups diced veal

1 cup mushrooms

½ onion

1 pint nonfalt milk

Cover veal with water and simmer the day before until water boils down to 1 quart of liquid. Next day, chop mushrooms and slice onions very fine. Simmer in stock and add milk. Heat and serve. Makes 2 one-cup servings of 110 calories each.

Macaroni and Cheese Bake

1 cup uncooked macaroni

1 tablespoon salt

3 quarts boiling water

2 tablespoons vegetable oil (except coconut oil)

2 tablespoons flour

2 cups nonfat milk

1 teaspoon salt

½ pound sharp cheese, grated

Add salt to rapidly boiling water in a large saucepan and drop in macaroni. Cook rapidly for about 20 minutes or until tender; drain. Run hot water through to rinse well. Melt fat in top of double boiler over boiling water, blend in flour, and add milk gradually, stirring until sauce is smooth and thick. Add salt and grated cheese and stir until cheese melts. Arrange hot macaroni and cheese in layers in greased casserole and bake in a moderately hot oven 10 to 15 minutes until brown on top. Makes 5 one-half cup servings of 125 calories.

Recipes: Day Three

Beef Broth Oriental

2 lbs. bony beef (bone & meat)
3 stalks celery with leaves cut up
2 medium carrots, cut up
1½ teaspoon salt
6 cups water
3 whole cloves
1 large onion cut into thirds

In stockpot or Dutch oven, combine beef pieces, celery, carrots, and salt. Add water. Push the cloves into each of the large onion thirds. Bring to boiling. Reduce heat, cover, and simmer about 1 hour or until beef is tender. Lift out beef pieces with slotted spoon. Strain stock through a sieve lined with 1 or 2 layers of cheesecloth; discard vegetables.

Clarify stock. Skim off fat with metal spoon or chill and lift off fat.

When beef is cool enough, lift meat from bones and save meat for another use. Makes about 5 one-cup servings of stock with 30 calories each. Store in refrigerator in covered container.

Use 1 cup of stock for beef broth. Add ½ cup of cooked rice to broth. As needed, the stock can be used for a variety of soups and stews.

Blueberry Coffeecake

4 eggs, separated
1 cup vegetable fat (except coconut oil)
2 cups sugar
2 cups sifted flour
1 teaspoon vanilla
1 cup blueberries, drained

Whip egg whites until stiff. In separate bowl, cream fat and sugar. Add egg yolks one at a time. Add flour and vanilla. Fold in egg whites and place in a greased pan 11″ × 16″ or ring-tube pan. Gently press in fruit. Bake 35 minutes at 350 degrees in flat pan. Top while hot with powdered sugar. Makes 8-10 servings of 135 calories each.

Scrambled Eggs Supreme

2 eggs
2 tablespoons nonfat milk
¼ teaspoon salt
1 tablespoon vegetable fat (except coconut oil)
½ cup mushrooms

Beat eggs just enough to mix yolks and whites. Stir in milk and salt. Melt fat in small frying pan and add egg mixture. Stir over low heat as eggs become firm, only enough to prevent eggs from sticking to pan; stir in mushrooms. Serve at once.

Scrambled eggs may also be prepared over hot water in a double boiler. They will take longer to cook and need not be stirred so frequently. They will be very delicate and tender when done. Makes one serving of 125 calories.

Cranberry Punch

1 quart fresh cranberries

1 quart water

1 cup sugar

5 whole cloves

1 teaspoon grated lemon rind

1 teaspoon grated orange rind

2 tablespoons lemon juice

1 quart apple juice

thin slices of orange

Cook cranberries and water in a covered kettle until skins pop. Purée berries, add sugar, cloves and rinds. Stir thoroughly. Chill. Add the lemons and apple juice and stir to blend. Garnish with thin slices of oranges. Serve immediately. Makes one-half cup servings of 60 calories each.

Fruit Cup Combination

Possible combination of fruits:

orange, grapefruit, pineapple

peach, orange, blackberries

apple, grapefruit, strawberries

grapes, orange, melon

melon, grapefruit, bananas

Sprinkle lightly with sugar. One-half cup mixed fruit contains 100 calories.

Lemonade

6 lemons

4 cups water

½-²⁄₃ cup sugar (to taste)

Squeeze the juice from the lemons and mix with the water and sugar. See that the sugar is well dissolved. Makes 6 one-cup serving of 75 calories each.

Tomato and Lettuce Salad

3 tomatoes

lettuce halves

6 tablespoons Italian dressing

Scald the tomatoes. Remove the skins and chill. Just before serving time, cut them in halves, crosswise and place one piece with the outside upward on each serving plate, with one or two leaves of crisp, white lettuce underneath. Pour over each portion a tablespoon of Italian dressing. One portion contains 125 calories.

Corn Syrup Lemonade

½ cup corn syrup

3 tablespoons lemon juice

½ cup water

Mix corn syrup with lemon juice until thoroughly blended. Add water and chill. Serve with a sprig of mint. Particularly suitable for raising calories on a low protein diet. Makes 1 one-cup serving with 75 calories.

Special French Dressing

½ teaspoon salt

⅛ teaspoon pepper

½ teaspoon sugar

½ teaspoon dry mustard

¼ teaspoon paprika

2 tablespoons vinegar

⅓ cup vegetable oil (except coconut oil)

Place all ingredients in a jar or in a bottle with a lip. Store in refrigerator. Shortly before serving, shake vigorously until the oil and vinegar blend to form a thick emulsion.

Variations: add herbs or other seasonings singly or in combination; catsup or chili sauce. (Crumble Roquefort/blue cheese and add or substitute grapefruit juice for vinegar and omit mustard for a fruit salad.) One tablespoon contains 30 calories.

Island Fruit Punch

3¾ cups pear halves quartered

3 cups unsweetened pineapple juice (canned)

1½ cups frozen lemonade concentrate, thawed

2 cups water

3½ cups lemon-lime carbonated beverage

Mix all ingredients except pears and lemon-lime carbonated beverage. Add pears. Add lemon-lime beverage and stir. Makes 24 one-half cup servings of 50 calories each.

Cream of Watercress Soup

4 medium-sized potatoes

1 tablespoon vegetable fat (except coconut oil)

salt

mace, if desired

1 cup nonfat milk

1 large bunch watercress

Boil potatoes in jackets, then skin and beat well with vegetable fat and seasoning. Add milk; smooth to consistency of heavy cream. Chop watercress fine without mashing; it must remain crisp. Now heat soup. Just before serving, drop in the watercress. Stir a moment until it is very hot but do not cook the watercress. Whatever is left over may be served cold in cups with a spoonful of sour cream on top. Makes 4 one-cup servings with 95 calories each.

Meatloaf With Herbs and Tomato Sauce

½ cup soft bread crumbs

1 pound ground beef

2 tablespoons grated onion

1 clove garlic finely chopped

¼ teaspoon oregano

¼ teaspoon basil

½ cup nonfat milk

1 egg, slightly beaten

2 tablespoons parsley, finely chopped

1 teaspoon salt

⅛ teaspoon rosemary

½ teaspoon paprika

Soak the bread crumbs in milk. Combine all ingredients and mix thoroughly. Place mixture in loaf pan. Bake for 1 hour in a moderate (350 degrees) oven. Serve hot or cold (slice thin if served cold). Tomato sauce may be used if served hot. Makes 4 4-ounce servings with 130 calories each.

Stuffed Baked Potato-Half Creole

6 baking potatoes

1 medium green pepper diced

⅓ cup vegetable oil (except coconut oil)

2 tablespoons instant minced onion

1 medium tomato diced

½ tablespoons nonfat milk

1 teaspoon paprika

¼ teaspoon crumbled whole rosemary leaves

Paprika for garnish

Wash potatoes. Dry. Bake in a preheated oven (450 degrees) 1 hour or until done. In the meantime, sauté green peppers with 3 tablespoons of fat until limp. Add onion and tomato and cook for 1 minute longer. Cut potatoes in half lengthwise and scoop out centers, leaving shells intact. Add milk and seasoning to potato centers and mash well. Blend in sautéed vegetables. Fill shells with mixture and dot tops with remaining fat. Bake in an oven preheated to 400 degrees for 20 minutes. Serve at once, garnishing with paprika. Makes 6 servings of 100 calories each.

Vegetable Soup

½ cup mixed vegetables: carrots, peas
½ cup cabbage, shredded
1 stalk celery, diced
½ cup tomato juice
salt and pepper
½ small onion, chopped
1 cup meat stock or bouillon cube and 1 cup water

Prepare vegetables and add to broth. Boil together until vegetables are just tender, about 20 minutes. Makes one serving with 100 calories.

Creamy Cucumber Dressing

1 cup finely chopped pared cucumber
½ cup chopped green pepper
1 clove garlic, finely chopped
½ teaspoon salt
½ cup yogurt (preferably homemade)
½ cup mayonnaise (Special)
½ cup chili sauce
1 tablespoon prepared horseradish
1 tablespoon lemon juice

Combine all ingredients in medium bowl. Mix well. Refrigerate 30 minutes or until well chilled. Makes 2 cups. (1 tablespoon has 20 calories.)

Fish Salad

7 oz. flaked, cooked fish (tuna or other flaked fish)
¼ cup oil
¼ cup pickle relish
½ cup chopped celery
lettuce
¼ cup mayonnaise (special)

The remains of almost any cold fish may be used in salad very satisfactorily, but the salad is more successful when made of fish that will flake nicely, such as salmon, cod, haddock, halibut, or tuna fish.

Remove the bones, pick the fish into flakes, turn over in oil mixed with pickle relish, and set away in a cold place. When about to serve, chop celery and add to the fish. Arrange crisp white leaves of lettuce in cup shapes on a platter, using one or two leaves for each, then lay one spoonful of the mixture in each cup and pour over it one teaspoonsful of mayonnaise. Makes 2 one-half cup servings with 135 calories each.

Creamy Potato Soup

4 slices bacon, cut up
3 medium potatoes, peeled and chopped (5 cups)
1 large onion, chopped (1 cup)
1 medium carrot, chopped (½ cup)
1 stalk celery, chopped (½ cup)
4 cups milk
2 teaspoons salt
2 tablespoons all-purpose flour
2 teaspoons paprika

In a large saucepan, cook bacon until crisp. Drain bacon, reserving 3 tablespoons drippings in pan. Set bacon aside. Add chopped potatoes, onion, carrot, and celery to bacon drippings. Cover and cook over low heat about 20 minutes, or until potatoes are tender, stirring occasionally. Stir in milk and salt; bring mixture to boiling.

Stir in flour added to enough milk to make a paste, add paprika. Cook and stir until mixture bubbles. Top with bacon pieces. Serve immediately. Makes 6-8 one cup servings of 145 calories each.

Sweet-Sour Tuna

1⅛ cups canned pineapple tidbits, drained
½ cup pineapple syrup
1 cup green pepper, cut in ½-inch pieces
¼ cup water chestnuts, sliced
1 tablespoon sugar
1 tablespoon cornstarch
1 teaspoon soy sauce
1 tablespoon vinegar
½ cup chicken broth (or chicken bouillon)
½ teaspoon salt
dash pepper
1 cup tuna, water-pack

Cook pineapple in lightly greased skillet for 5 minutes. Add pineapple syrup, green pepper, and water chestnuts. Cover and simmer for 10 minutes. Combine sugar, cornstarch, soy sauce, vinegar, chicken broth, and seasonings. Add to pineapple. Cook, stirring constantly until thickened. Add tuna. Heat thoroughly. Serve over boiled rice. Makes 6 one-half cup servings of 135 calories each.

Raisin Bread

1 cup whole-wheat flour
3-4 cups unbleached flour
½ cup sugar
1 teaspoon salt
2 packets active dry yeast
1 cup nonfat milk
⅓ cup water
2 tablespoons honey
½ cup vegetable oil (except coconut oil)
1 egg
1½ cup medium raisins
2 teaspoons cinnamon
½ teaspoon nutmeg

In a large mixing bowl, combine whole wheat flour, 1 cup of unbleached flour, sugar, salt, and yeast. Put milk, water, honey, and fat in a saucepan. Place over low heat, stirring. When liquid is almost hot to the touch (120-130 degrees) remove from heat. Gradually add milk mixture to dry ingredients, beating at low speed. Add egg and beat at medium speed for 2 minutes. Add 1 cup of white flour, stir in well and beat batter at high speed for 2 minutes. Stir in enough additional flour to produce a stiff batter. Cover, let rise in a warm place (80-85 degrees) until double in bulk, about 1 hour. Stir batter down. With a spoon beat in raisins and spices. Turn batter into two greased 1-quart casseroles. Bake immediately at 350 degrees for 40 to 45 minutes. Remove loaves from casseroles and serve immediately. Makes 2 loaves. (A one-half inch slice has 80 calories.)

Cheese Souffle

2 tablespoons vegetable fat (except coconut oil)
2 tablespoons flour
¼ teaspoon salt
½ cup nonfat milk
¼ pound (1 cup) Cheddar cheese grated
2 egg yolks
2 egg whites, stiffly beaten

Melt fat in a small saucepan. Stir in flour and salt. When smooth, stir in milk gradually. Remove from heat, add cheese, and stir until melted. Stir in egg yolks one at a time, beating after each addition. Fold into stiffly-beaten egg whites. Pour into greased 1-pint casserole and bake in slow oven (300 degrees) 1 hour or in moderately hot oven (425 degrees) for 25 minutes. Makes 2 one cup servings of 135 calories each.

Baking-Powder Biscuits

2 cups flour
4 teaspoons baking powder
1 teaspoon salt
2 tablespoons vegetable fat (except coconut oil)
½ cup liquid nonfat milk

Mix dry ingredients and sift twice. Mix in fat with tips of fingers, or cut in with two knives. Add liquid gradually, mixing with a knife until soft dough forms. It is not always possible to determine the exact amount of liquid, due to differences in flours. Toss on a floured board. Pat and roll slightly to one-inch thickness. Shape with a biscuit-cutter. Bake in hot oven (450-460 degrees) for 12-15 minutes. Makes 12 biscuits with 75 calories each.

Bill's Special Ambrosia

3 fresh oranges
3 fresh grapefruit
½ small fresh pineapple
½ cup orange juice
½ cup light corn syrup
½ cup flaked or fresh coconut, shredded

Peel and section oranges and grapefruit. Peel and dice pineapple and mix with orange and grapefruit sections. Combine orange juice and syrup. Divide fruit mixture into 6 sherbet glasses. Pour juice over fruit and top with coconut. Other fruits may be added in season. Makes 6 one-half cup servings of 110 calories each.

Cheese-Topped Stuffed Tomato Half

6 medium-sized tomatoes, washed
½ cup soft bread crumbs rolled in melted fat
salt to taste
½ cup cooked meat (chicken/tuna fish) (Mushrooms may be used to replace meat)
¼ cup grated cheddar cheese

Cut a thin slice from stem end of each tomato and remove pulp. Mix with meat (or mushrooms), soft bread crumbs, vegetable fat, and seasoning. Fill tomato shells with mixture. Cover tops with bread crumbs that have been mixed with the melted vegetable fat and cheese. Bake at 375 degrees for 30 minutes or until tender. Makes 6 servings of 75 calories each (with mushrooms); 95 calories each (with meat).

Baked Apples

1 apple, red medium size
1 cinnamon red heart
2 teaspoons sugar
½ cup water

Select sound apples. Core them, add cinnamon red-heart to each center, and place 1 teaspoon to 1 tablespoon sugar in each cavity. Place apples on a baking dish. Add water to cover bottom of dish. Bake in moderate oven (350-375 degrees) until tender.

Sour apples cook more quickly than sweet ones, and summer or fall apples take less time to cook than do winter apples.

Baked apples may be varied by filling the centers with brown sugar and raisins, sections of bananas, red cinnamon candies, marshmallow, marmalade or jelly, honey or corn syrup and lemon juice, nuts, candied orange peel, candied pineapple, preserved ginger, canned or fresh berries, peaches and other fruits, or left-over fruit juice. Meringue or custard sauce may be used as garnish. One apple contains 125 calories.

Stuffed Peaches

Pare large peaches and cut a slice from the top of each. Remove the pits without breaking the fruit and fill the hollow with nuts or with any chopped fruit, such as apples, citron or raisins. Sprinkle with sugar and a little cinnamon or nutmeg. Pour custard over the peaches and bake or serve cold custard with the uncooked chilled fruit. Two stuffed halves contain 110 calories.

Roast Turkey

1 roasting turkey

salt

stuffing*

vegetable oil (except coconut oil)

flour

Wash, singe, and drain the bird. Rub it with salt, inside and out, and stuff with desired dressing. Truss and tie the fowl. Brush skin with melted or softened fat. Turn breast side down and cover bird with a cloth dipped in fat. Place in pan large enough for bird. Place in a moderate oven (325-350 degrees). Cook uncovered, breast-side down, about one-half of total time. Turn breast up. Place any of body fat removed in dressing over breastbone. Bake with extra vegetable fat. (The cloth may be removed toward end of cooking if bird is not well-browned.) Allow 30 minutes per pound for small, 25 minutes per pound for large bird. One 4-ounce serving contains 125 calories.

*Cornbread Stuffing

5 cups crumbled cornbread

6 cups white bread

1½ cups onion

1-1½ cups celery, chopped

½ cup nonfat (skim) milk

1 egg

1 cup chicken stock

Toss together about 5 cups crumbled cornbread and 6 cups white bread (not too fresh). Add 1½ cups onion and 1½-2 cups celery chopped and cooked slightly in ½ cup nonfat milk. Mix in 1 egg, slightly beaten, and 1 cup stock. Cook in greased baking dish about 30 minutes at 350 degrees. Makes 12 one-half-cup servings of 100 calories each.

*Sage Dressing

2 large sandwich loaves of bread thoroughly dried and ground in grinder

2 cups minced celery

1 cup minced onion

¼ cup vegetable fat melted (except coconut oil)

1 teaspoon each salt and pepper

2 teaspoons sage

Combine ingredients. Moisten with water. Bake in greased baking dish about 350 degrees for about 30 minutes. Makes 10-12 one-half cup servings of 95 calories each.

Tossed Salad

½ head lettuce

4 leaves spinach

4 leaves watercress

1 green pepper (small)

2 carrots

2 stalks celery

2 radishes

1 tomato

lemon slices

bread cubes

2 slices crisp bacon

salad dressing (your favorite)

Chop lettuce into lettuce lined bowl. Chop spinach and watercress leaves. Cube green pepper, carrots (sliced round) and celery. Mix thoroughly. Slice radishes and place on top. Quarter tomato for top garnish. Serve with lemon slices, bread cubes, and 2 slices crisp, cooked bacon chopped into fine bits. Add your favorite dressing. Makes one one-cup serving with 150 calories.

Date-Nut Rolls

1 stick vegetable fat (except coconut oil)
1 cup diced dates
1 cup chopped nuts
1 cup granulated sugar
⅛ teaspoon salt
1 teaspoon vanilla
1½ cups crisp cereal
1 cup powdered sugar

Mix first 5 ingredients in saucepan and cook 8 minutes at low heat. Remove from heat. Add vanilla and crisp cereal. Shape into finger-size rolls. Roll in powdered sugar. Makes 24 rolls with 100 calories each.

Baked Custard

3 eggs
¼ to ½ cup sugar
few grains salt
½ teaspoon vanilla or sprinkling of nutmeg
2 cups nonfat milk, scalded

Beat the eggs slightly; beat in the sugar, salt, and vanilla. Stir in the hot milk; pour into individual molds of oven glassware or earthenware. Set molds into a pan, pour hot water nearly to top of molds. Bake in moderate oven (350 degrees) for about 45 minutes. The custard is done when a knife inserted in the center comes out clean. Makes 6 one-half cup servings of 180 calories each.

Milk Toast

2 cups nonfat (skim) milk
2 white bread slices, toasted and spread with 1 teaspoon vegetable fat (except coconut oil)

Heat milk in small saucepan just until bubbles form around edge of pan. Remove from heat; let cool slightly. Serve toast slices in individual soup plates with ¼ cup warm milk poured over each. Makes 2 servings of 160 calories each.

Variations:

Cinnamon-Sugar Milk Toast: Combine 2 teaspoons sugar with ½ teaspoon cinnamon, mixing well. Proceed as directed for Milk Toast, sprinkling toast slices with cinnamon-sugar mixture. Makes 2 servings of 200 calories each.

Banana Milk Toast: Proceed as directed for Milk Toast, arranging a few banana slices over each toast slice. Makes 2 servings with 200 calories each.

or, **Make It Simple:** 1 glass cold milk, whole or nonfat, 1 slice toast, cubed. Mix together and eat with spoon. Makes 1 serving with 160 calories.

Egg Salad on Toast

6 hard-cooked eggs
salt, dash
¼ cup chopped pickle
10 slices bread
1 teaspoon prepared mustard
mayonnaise (special)

Shell eggs and chop rather fine. Mix with salt, pickle, and mustard. Add just enough mayonnaise to give a good spreading consistency. Spread on half the slices of bread. Top with remaining slices. Cut sandwiches in thirds. Makes 5 servings of 160 calories each.

Additional Recipes for Variety

Soups

A soup or stew can be prepared for any part of the meal. It can become a great stress reliever when served hot and full of many nutrients. A glass of milk will often complete the needed nutrition for the meal, especially if you are following the six-meal diet plan.

Try these soups and stews to add variety to your menus.

Wonton Soup

1 beaten egg
¼ cup finely chopped onion
¼ cup chopped water chestnuts
1 tablespoon soy sauce
2 teaspoons grated fresh gingeroot
½ teaspoon sugar
¼ teaspoon salt
½ lb. ground pork
½ cup shrimp drained and deveined
40 wonton skins or 10 eggroll skins, cut in quarters
8 cups water
6 cups chicken broth (see Beef Broth, page 45)
1 cup thinly sliced mushrooms
½ cup pea pods
½ cup thinly sliced bamboo shoots
4 green onions, sliced in ½-inch lengths

For filling: in a bowl, combine egg, onion, water chestnuts, soy sauce, gingeroot, sugar, and salt. Add ground pork and chopped shrimp. Mix well.

Position a wonton skin with one point toward you. Spoon 1 rounded teaspoon of filling just below center of skin. Fold bottom point of wonton skin over filling, tuck point under filling. Roll up skin and filling, leaving about 1 inch at top of skin. Moisten the right hand corner of skin with water. Grasp the two lower corners of triangle, then bring these corners toward you below the filling. Overlap the left corner over the right-hand corner; press and seal. Use 20 for soup. Freeze the remainder for future use.

In a large saucepan, bring the 8 cups of water to boiling. Drop wontons one at a time into boiling water. Simmer uncovered for 3 minutes. Remove from heat and rinse with cold water; drain well.

In the same saucepan, bring chicken broth (recipe on p. 45) to boiling. Add mushrooms, pea pods, bamboo shoots, and the pre-cooled wontons. Simmer uncovered for 4 to 5 minutes. Stir in green onions. Ladle soup into individual soup bowls. Makes 20 one-cup servings with 110 calories each.

Celery-Spinach Soup

1 cup chicken broth
1 cup spinach
2 cups chopped celery
1 cup chopped onion
1 cup cream-style cottage cheese
2 cups milk
½ teaspoon salt

In 3-quart saucepan combine chicken broth, spinach, celery, and onion. Bring to boiling. Reduce heat. Cover and simmer 10 minutes or until vegetables are tender. Transfer to blender and add cottage cheese. Cover and blend until smooth. Return mixture to saucepan. Stir in milk and salt. Heat through. Serve in soup bowls. Makes 6 one-cup servings of 100 calories each. Oysters may be substituted for celery.

Mist of Cantaloupe

1 medium cantaloupe
½ teaspoon ground cinnamon
1 tablespoon lime juice
1 cup orange juice concentrate
1½ cups water

Cut cantaloupe in half and remove seeds. Scoop pulp into blender. Add cinnamon. Cover and blend until smooth. Turn into large bowl. In same blender, place lime juice, orange juice and water. Cover and blend until mixed. Stir into melon mixture. Stir before serving. Cover and chill thoroughly. Garnish with fresh mint leaves or wedges of lime. Makes 6-8 one-cup servings of 100 calories each.

Creamy Cucumber Soup

3 medium cucumbers, peeled, seeded and chopped (3 cups)
1 small onion, chopped (¼ cup)
3 tablespoons vegetable fat (except coconut oil)
¼ cup all-purpose flour
3 cups chicken broth* (See recipe p. 45)
1 cup whipping cream

In 2-quart saucepan, cook cucumbers and onion, covered in vegetable fat, for about 15 minutes or until tender. Stir–in flour. Add chicken broth (recipe on page 45) and whipping cream, cook, and stir until thickened and bubbly. Pour half of mixture into blender. Blend until smooth. Set aside. Repeat with remaining mixture. Cover and chill. Garnish with cucumber slices. Makes 10-12 one-cup servings of 125 calories each.

Cheese Soup

½ cup vegetable fat (except coconut oil)
½ cup all-purpose flour
4 cups nonfat milk
4 cups shredded cheddar cheese
3 cups water
1 cup diced celery
2 cups diced potato, peeled
1 cup diced carrots
½ cup diced onion
¾ teaspoon salt

Melt vegetable fat in a heavy, 2-quart saucepan over low heat. Add flour, stirring until smooth. Cook 1 minute, stirring constantly. Gradually stir in nonfat milk. Cook over medium heat, stirring constantly until thickened. Add cheese, stirring until cheese is melted. Remove from heat and set aside.

Combine water, vegetables, and salt in a 5-quart, heavy-duty Dutch oven and heat to boiling. Reduce heat and cover; simmer 10 minutes or until vegetables are tender. Stir in cheese mixture, cook over low heat (350 degrees) until thoroughly heated. Makes 10-12 one-cup servings of 160 calories each.

Pumpkin Soup

1 lb. meaty beef short ribs
4 cups water
8 oz. pumpkin, peeled, cubed, and cut up (about 3 cups)
1 medium potato, peeled and quartered
1 large carrot, quartered
½ cup onion, finely chopped
½ cup milk
1½ teaspoons salt

In a 4-quart Dutch oven or large saucepan, brown short ribs over low heat (add some cooking oil if needed). Add water, bring to boiling. Reduce heat, cover, and simmer 1 hour.

Remove ribs from broth. When ribs are cool enough to handle, cut meat from bone and return meat to broth.

Add pumpkin, potato, carrot, onion, and salt to broth. Cover and simmer over medium heat (350 degrees) for 45 minutes.

Pour half of mixture into blender and blend until smooth. Return blended mixture to saucepan. Repeat with balance of mixture. Add milk. Heat through. Pour into soup bowls. Makes 6 one-cup servings of 160 calories each.

Meat Stock or Broth

1 2½ or 3 pound chicken or
  3 pounds brisket, shinbone, or other soup meat
  and bone

1 tablespoon salt
3 quarts cold water
2 cups vegetables (carrot, celery, onion)
¾ cup tomatoes
½ green peppers

For plain broth, leave off vegetables.

Sprinkle meat and bone with salt. Let stand for 1 hour. Add water and soak ½ hour. Simmer 3½ hours uncovered. Add remaining ingredients and simmer, covered, ½ hour. Strain. Chill and remove the fat. Variations may be made by substituting chicken or veal for beef. This is a standard method for making soup stock. The fat content will be negligible if the stock is chilled and the fat removed as directed. Makes one gallon with 30 calories each cup.

Fruit Cream Soup

2½ cups frozen, thawed raspberries, blueberries,   strawberries, peaches, or mixed fruit
1 cup water
¼ cup sugar
2 inches cinnamon stick
Dash ground nutmeg
Dash ground cloves
1 tablespoon water
1 tablespoon cornstarch
2 tablespoons lemon juice
1 cup sour cream
½ cup milk

Drain fruit, reserving syrup (cut up large pieces of fruit). In 1½-quart saucepan, combine reserved syrup, the 1 cup of water, sugar, cinnamon, nutmeg, and cloves. Bring to boiling, reduce heat, and simmer uncovered for 5 minutes. Blend 1 tablespoon water with cornstarch, stir into saucepan. Cook and stir until thickened and bubbly. Remove from heat. Add lemon juice, cool to room temperature. Blend in sour cream and fruit. Stir in milk. Cover and chill. Garnish with lemon peel. Makes 4-6 one-cup servings of 130 calories each.

Main Dishes

Ragout of Beef

3 tablespoons all-purpose flour
2¼ teaspoons salt
½ teaspoon paprika
1½ lbs. stewing beef, cut in 1-inch cubes
2 tablespoons olive oil
2 garlic cloves, finely chopped
2 tablespoons chopped parsley
1 cup beef broth
¾ cup dry red wine
½ bay leaf
4 cups small whole onions
2 tablespoons tomato paste
1 cup macaroni
1 tablespoon vegetable fat

In a medium bowl, combine flour, 1½ teaspoon salt, and paprika. Add beef cubes and toss until well–coated with seasoned flour. In a heavy pan, heat oil. Add beef cubes and brown on all sides. Add garlic and parsley and cook one minute. Stir in beef broth, wine, bay leaf, and remaining ¾ teaspoon salt. Bring all to boil, cover and simmer 1½ hours, stirring.

Add onions and tomato paste. Cover and continue simmering about 15 minutes. Remove cover and simmer until meat is tender and sauce has thickened, about 20 minutes. Discard bay leaf.

Cook macaroni in large saucepan. Drain and mix with vegetable fat. Place macaroni around the outer edges of a platter to form a ring. Spoon beef mixture into center of macaroni circle. Sprinkle sauce over macaroni and beef mixture or serve sauce separately. Makes 6 8-ounce servings with 130 calories each.

Oriental Beef Balls

1 lb. ground beef
¼ cup cornstarch, divided
2 tablespoons vegetable oil
3 tablespoons vinegar
½ cup sugar
2 small green peppers, chopped
1 egg
1 teaspoon salt
2 tablespoons chopped onion
2 cups pineapple chunks
¼ cup and 2 tablespoons water
3 tablespoons soy sauce

Combine beef, egg, 1 tablespoon cornstarch, salt, onion and pepper. Shape into 1-inch balls. Brown in 2 tablespoons hot oil in medium skillet; drain. Drain pineapple, add additional water, if necessary, to make 1 cup. Combine 3 tablespoons cornstarch, soy sauce, vinegar, water and sugar. Add to pineapple juice and cook until mixture has thickened, stirring constantly. Add meatballs, pineapple, and green peppers. Heat throughly. Makes 6 servings with 130 calories each.

This recipe can be used for an hors d'oeuvre or entree (served over rice).

Broiled Haddock Fillet

1 lb. haddock fillets
salt to taste
3 tablespoons vegetable fat
1 onion, minced
2 tablespoons catsup
1 tablespoon Worcestershire sauce
bacon slices cooked crisp
orange slices
pecan halves

Place haddock on rack of broiler pan and sprinkle with salt. Melt the vegetable fat in a saucepan and add the onion, catsup, and Worcestershire sauce. Stir until well blended, then spoon over the haddock. Broil about 15 minutes on each side, basting with the onion mixture. Garnish with nuts, crisp bacon, and orange slices. Makes 4 4-ounce servings with 125 calories each.

Scallops Gingered

1½ lbs. scallops, sliced thinly
6 tablespoons vegetable fat
1 teaspoon salt
2 tablespoons fresh ginger, minced or powdered
2 tablespoons parsley, finely chopped

Place sliced scallops in baking dish. Add vegetable fat, melted. Add salt sprinkling over scallops. Add ginger in the same manner. Top with parsley. Place dish in 350 degree oven and bake until slightly browned, about 15-20 minutes. Makes 6 4-ounce servings with 125 calories each.

Teriyaki Steak

½ cup soy sauce
2 tablespoons sugar
1 clove garlic, crushed
¼ cup dry white wine
½ teaspoon ginger, ground
2 lbs. sirloin steak or rib steak, cut ½-inch thick

Combine first 5 ingredients and stir to dissolve sugar. Place steak in heavy-duty plastic bag; pour marinade over steak. Secure plastic bag, making sure marinade covers the pieces of meat. Place on refrigerator tray for 15 minutes. Remove steak from sauce and place meat in heat-proof dish. Broil 2½ minutes on each side for medium-rare, 3 minutes each side for medium-well. Makes 6 4-ounce servings with 150 calories each.

Steak may be grilled by removing from dish and placing on grill.

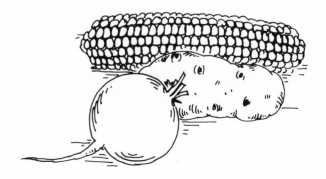

Swiss Omelet Roll

1 cup mayonnaise

2 tablespoons chopped green onion

2 tablespoons pure prepared mustard

½ cup mayonnaise

2 tablespoons flour

1 cup milk

12 eggs separated

1½ cups finely chopped ham

1 cup shredded Swiss cheese

¼ cup chopped green onion

watercress

Combine first three ingredients. Mix well. Set aside for top dressing.

Combine mayonnaise and flour. Gradually add milk and beaten egg yolk; cook, stirring constantly over low heat until thickened. Remove from heat, cool for 15 minutes. Fold mayonnaise mixture and seasonings into stiffly beaten egg whites. Pour into 15″ × ½″ × 10″ ½-inch jelly-roll pan lined with wax paper and brushed with mayonnaise. Bake at 425 degrees 20 minutes. Invert pan on towel carefully and remove wax paper. Cover with combined ham, cheese, and green onion. Roll from narrow end, lifting with towel while rolling; make a roll. Serve with seam down, top with mustard sauce. Garnish with watercress. Makes 6-8 servings of 140 calories each.

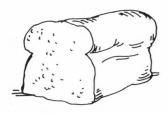

Pineapple-Baked Chicken

1 2½ to 3 lb. fryer

1 teaspoon poultry seasoning

¼ teaspoon salt

1½ cup soft bread crumbs

⅓ cup flaked coconut

¼ cup finely chopped celery

¼ cup drained crushed pineapple

1 tablespoon grated orange peel

6 tablespoons melted vegetable fat

¼ cup pineapple juice

½ cup water

2 tablespoons meat sauce

¼ cup orange juice

Rinse the chicken with cold water and drain. Rub cavity with poultry seasoning and salt. Combine the bread crumbs, coconut, celery, pineapple, orange peel, and 2 tablespoons butter in a bowl and stir lightly to blend. Place in cavity of chicken and truss. Brush chicken with 3 tablespoons vegetable fat. Place rack in roasting pan and add water. Cover. Bake in 375 degree oven for about 1 hour.

Combine remaining vegetable fat with remaining ingredients. Uncover chicken and brush with half of the orange-pineapple mixture. Bake for about 30 additional minutes, brushing frequently with remaining orange-pineapple mixture.

Serve on platter. Garnish with pineapple rings and grape clusters. Makes 4-5 4-ounce servings with 140 calories each.

Cheese-Tuna Loaf

1 tablespoon vegetable fat
12 slices bread
3 cups tuna fish
¾ lb. grated Cheddar cheese
4 eggs, beaten
3 cups milk
¼ teaspoon salt

Spread vegetable fat on one side of each bread slice. Place 6 slices, fat side down, in 9″ × 13″ pan. Drain and flake tuna. Spread tuna over bread and sprinkle cheese over tuna. Place remaining slices of bread, fat side up, on cheese. Mix the eggs, milk, and salt and pour over bread. Let stand for 1 hour. Bake in 350 degree oven for 35 minutes or until lightly browned. Makes 6 one-half-cup servings of 135 calories each.

Mushroom Rice

3 cups hot, cooked rice cooked in chicken broth
½ cup sliced mushrooms, drained
1 cup cooked green peas
2 tablespoons vegetable fat, melted
¼ teaspoon onion powder
salt to taste
1 tablespoon diced pimento

Combine rice, mushrooms, peas, vegetable fat, seasonings, and pimento. Heat until vegetables are hot — about 3 to 4 minutes. Toss lightly. Makes 6 one-half-cup servings with 110 calories each.

Vegetable Dishes

Stuffed Carrots

6 large carrots, scraped, boiled, and drained
2 cups cheddar cheese, shredded
1 teaspoon sugar
1 teaspoon Worcestershire sauce
mayonnaise
bread crumbs rolled in melted vegetable fat

Scoop out more than half of cooked carrots, leaving a shell. Mix together cheddar cheese, sugar, and Worcestershire sauce. Add enough mayonnaise to make a paste and stuff carrot shells. Cover with bread crumbs and bake at 325 degrees about 15 minutes. Makes 6 one-half-cup servings with 130 calories each.

Asparagus Casserole

2 tablespoons vegetable fat (except coconut oil)
1 tablespoon all-purpose flour
1 teaspoon salt
1½ lbs. fresh asparagus spears cooked (liquid reserved)
½ cup evaporated milk
½ cup cornflake crumbs
2 hard-cooked eggs, chopped
½ cup shredded Cheddar cheese

Melt vegetable fat in saucepan. Stir in flour and salt. Add asparagus liquid to evaporate milk to make 1½ cups, stir in flour mixture and blend until smooth. Cook sauce for 2 minutes. Spread asparagus spears in bottom of greased, shallow 2-quart casserole. Sprinkle half of crumbs over asparagus, add eggs and half of the sauce. Add remaining crumbs, then the remaining sauce. Sprinkle with Cheddar cheese. Bake at 350 degrees for 30 minutes or until bubbly. Makes 4-6 one-half-cup servings with 110 calories each.

Applesauced Baked Squash

4 medium-sized acorn squash
1 lb. bulk pork sausage
1 teaspoon ground cinnamon
2 cups apple sauce
⅛ teaspoon salt

Scrub squash; cut in half lengthwise, removing seeds and stringy fiber. Place cut-side down on a baking sheet. Bake at 350 degrees about 40 minutes, or until almost tender. Form sausage into 24 small balls and brown in skillet. Drain.

Combine cinnamon and applesauce. Turn squash cut-side up, salt cavity and fill with apple sauce mixture. Place 3 sausage balls on top of apple sauce. Return to oven for 20 minutes. Makes 8 one-half-cup servings with 160 calories each.

Almondine Whole Green Beans

4 cups water
1½ teaspoon salt
3 lbs. fresh whole green beans
1 cup slivered almonds
¼ cup vegetable fat, melted (except coconut oil)
2 tablespoons lemon juice

Bring water and salt to a boil in a large saucepan. Add beans. Cook, covered, for 8 minutes or until tender. Drian well.

Sauté almonds in vegetable fat. Stir in lemon juice, toss with the beans. Serve very hot. Makes 6 one-half-cup servings with 105 calories each.

Broccoli, Herbed

3 lbs. broccoli
3 chicken bouillon cubes
2 cups boiling water
¼ cup chopped onion
1 teaspoon marjoram
1 teaspoon basil
3 tablespoons melted vegetable fat

Wash broccoli well, removing large leaves and cutting off ends and stalks. Cut large stalks in half lengthwise. Dissolve bouillon cubes in water in a large skillet. Add onion, marjoram, basil, and broccoli. Cover, then cook quickly for about 10 minutes or until just tender. Drain. Add vegetable fat. Makes 6 one-half-cup servings with 110 calories each.

Stuffed Green Peppers

6 medium-sized green peppers
vegetable fat
2 cups cooked ground meat (beef or ham)
¾ cup gravy or bouillon
1 cup cooked rice
1 teaspoon salt
3 tablespoons minced onions

Wash peppers and cut off a slice from the top of each pepper; remove the seeds. Parboil for 2 minutes. Drain and rub outer skins with shortening. Combine remaining ingredients and fill the peppers. Place in baking dish and bake at 350 degrees for 45 minutes. Makes 6 servings with 120 calories each.

Leftover roast beef or baked ham with gravy make excellent stuffings.

Stuffed Cucumbers

4 medium cucumbers, peeled and diced

cucumber pulp (from 2 cucumbers)

1 medium onion, chopped, divided

2 medium tomatoes, diced and divided

¾ cup dry bread crumbs

1½ teaspoon salt

12 slices bacon, cooked and crumbled

¼ cup water

½ cup vegetable fat

Cut each cucumber lengthwise into 2 sections; scrape out inside. Mix cucumber pulp with half the onion, diced tomato, bread crumbs, salt, and 5 slices bacon, crumbled.

Fill cucumber shells with mixture. Place remaining crumbled bacon, onion, and tomato into 1-quart casserole. Put stuffed cucumbers on top. Pour water around cucumbers, dot tops with vegetable fat. Bake at 350 degrees 45 minutes to 1 hour until cucumbers are tender. Makes 8 one-half cup servings with 100 calories each.

Shrimp-Stuffed Mushrooms

1½ lbs. fresh mushrooms, washed and dried

4 tablespoons melted vegetable fat

¼ cup chopped onion

½ cup tiny shrimp, drained

1 tablespoon mustard

¼ teaspoon lemon juice

¼ cup mayonnaise

1 hard-cooked egg, finely chopped

¼ teaspoon salt

Remove stems from mushrooms (save for soups or stews). Heat melted fat in large skillet. Add mushroom caps and sauté for 5 minutes, turning occasionally. Remove mushrooms to baking pan, cap-side up; set aside. Sauté onion in same skillet. Add remaining ingredients and mix well. Fill sautéed mushroom caps with shrimp mixture. Bake at 450 degrees for 6 to 8 minutes. Serve hot. Yield: about 30 mushrooms with 30 calories each.

Spinach, Creamed

2 tablespoons finely chopped onions

2 tablespoons hot bacon drippings

2 tablespoons all-purpose flour

1 cup light cream

4 cups fresh cooked, chopped spinach

1 teaspoon salt

¼ teaspoon ground nutmeg

Sauté onions in hot bacon drippings until golden brown. Blend in flour. Add light cream and stir with a wire whisk or fork until thickened. Add spinach and seasonings and blend thoroughly. Makes 4 one-half-cup servings with 130 calories each.

Onions Baked and Stuffed

6 medium onions

3 tablespoons vegetable fat

½ teaspoon leaf marjoram, crumbled

½ teaspoon salt

2 tablespoons grated Parmesan cheese

salt

2 tablespoons chopped parsley

1 cup (2 slices) soft bread crumbs

1 tablespoon finely-diced pimento

Cut tops off onions, peel. Remove centers, leaving a shell ½- to ¾-inch thick. Sprinkle insides of onion with salt. Chop half the onion removed from centers. Sauté in 2 tablespoons vegetable fat. Add parsley, marjoram, bread crumbs, pimento, ½ teaspoon salt, and cheese. Spoon into onion shells. Brush with remaining vegetable fat. Place in 1½-quart casserole; cover. Bake at 400 degrees for 45 to 50 minutes or until tender. Makes 6 servings with 110 calories each.

Tomato and Celery Sauté

2 large tomatoes, peeled, halved, and seeded

1 bunch green onions

¼ cup finely chopped parsley

4 tablespoons vegetable fat

3 cups thinly sliced celery and tops

½ teaspoon salt

Peel tomatoes, cut in halves, and gently squeeze to remove seeds. Dice tomatoes and set aside. Slice green onions, including part of tips. Remove. Combine onions and parsley.

Heat vegetable fat in frying pan over high heat until it starts to bubble. Add celery and cook for 7 minutes, then add onion mixture. Sprinkle with salt and stir gently for 3 minutes. Remove from heat, cover pan, and serve. Makes 6 one-half cup servings with 100 calories each.

Salads and Salad Dressings

Sautéed Cucumber

2 tablespoons vegetable fat
2 scallions, trimmed and finely sliced
2 medium cucumbers, peeled, seeded
¼ teaspoon salt
4 teaspoons sour cream
2 tablespoons chopped chives

Heat 1 tablespoon vegetable fat in skillet until bubbling. Add scallions to skillet and sauté them gently for about 1 minute. Add the remaining vegetable fat and cucumber slices and sauté, shaking pan to cook slices evenly.

When cucumber slices begin to lose water (after 2 minutes) season with salt, stir in sour cream, and sprinkle with chives. Cook until sour cream is warm but do not boil. Makes 5 one-half cup servings with 105 calories each.

Orange and Spinach Salad

2 bunches spinach
1 small bunch watercress
½-1 teaspoon dried summer savory
1 orange, peeled and divided into segments
1 orange cut finely, and juice

Wash and drain spinach and trim of any tough stems. Divide the bunches into large and small leaves. Save the leaves for use later. Tear small leaves into bite-sized pieces and place in bowl with watercress and savory. Scatter the orange segments on top and sprinkle on juice and finely-cut pieces. Mix with dressing. Makes 8 one-half cup servings with 80 calories each.

Caesar Seafood Salad

6 cups torn salad greens
¾ cup croutons
1 peeled avocado, diced
½ cup crab meat
¾ cup small cooked shrimp
¾ cup sliced boiled lobster tails
1 tomato
¾ cup Caesar dressing

Place salad greens in salad bowl, then add croutons. Combine the avocado and seafood and place in center of bowl. Cut the tomato in wedges and arrange around the edges. Add the dressing just before serving and toss lightly. Iceberg lettuce, Boston lettuce or romaine may be used for the salad greens. Makes 6 one-half cup servings with 130 calories each.

Mushroom and Fresh-Spinach Salad

1 lb. fresh spinach, torn
6 slices bacon, cooked and crumbled
⅔ cup sliced fresh mushrooms
½ cup fresh tomatoes, diced
6 cucumber wedges

Combine spinach, mushrooms, bacon, and tomatoes in large salad bowl; toss lightly; serve on salad plates with cucumber wedges on each. Pour Special Italian dressing over each serving. Makes 6 one-half cup servings with 110 calories each.

Chicken and Fruit Salad

1 5-lb. chicken
4 cups water with 2 teaspoons salt
¾ cup diced celery
1 cup seedless white grapes
1 cup mandarin orange sections
½ cup mayonnaise
½ cup sour cream
2 tablespoons finely minced onion
chopped parsley
1 tablespoon lemon juice
½ teaspoon salt
lettuce
¼ cup toasted almond slivers

Cook chicken in salted water until tender. Drain and cool. Remove skin. Remove chicken from bones and cut in pieces. Place in a bowl and add celery. Cut the grapes in half and add to chicken mixture. Drain the orange sections and add to chicken mixture. Mix the mayonnaise, sour cream, onion, parsley, lemon juice, and salt and pour over chicken mixture. Mix well and cover. Chill for several hours. Serve on lettuce. Sprinkle with almond slivers. Serves 6-8 one-half cup servings with 145 calories each.

Note: Sliced banana, 1 cup pineapple, and ¼ cup to ½ cup sliced olives can be substituted in this recipe to make banana-chicken salad.

Salad Dressing

¼ cup olive oil
1 tablespoon lemon rind, grated
1 clove garlic, minced
2 tablespoons lemon juice
salt (dash)
1 teaspoon oregano or thyme
1 tablespoon Parmesan cheese, grated

Combine all ingredients, mix well, and shake before using. Store in covered jar or bottle. Makes 4 one-tablespoon servings of 30 calories each.

Fresh Fruit, Garden Greens with Mushrooms

1 cup hand-picked lettuce
¼ pear, cut in four slices
¼ apple cut in four slices
2 large mushrooms, sliced
cherry tomato
chopped parsley
vinaigrette dressing

Place lettuce in center of salad plate. Arrange pear, apple, and mushroom slices around greens. Cut cherry tomato in half and place on top of greens. Sprinkle with parsley. Serve with vinaigrette dressing. Makes 1 salad with 110 calories.

Special Mayonnaise

½ teaspoon plain gelatin

2 egg yolks

2 tablespoons sugar

1 teaspoon salt

1½ cups powdered nonfat milk

1½ teaspoons dry mustard

¼ cup mild vinegar

Soak gelatin in ¼ cup cold milk. Scald 1¼ cups milk in double boiler. Remove from fire and dissolve gelatin in it. Beat together egg yolks, sugar, dry mustard, and salt. Stir into egg a little of the hot milk and gelatin mixture. Blend and add remainder of milk mixture. Return these ingredients to double boiler and cook, stirring over a very low flame until they begin to thicken (about 10 minutes). Remove from fire. Add vinegar slowly. This will still be a comparatively thin mixture, which thickens as it cools. If any lumps of gelatin remain, strain while pouring into jar for storage. Allow to cool and then refrigerate. This dressing is fine for coleslaw. If you usually thin your mayonnaise with vinegar when using it on slaw, you can do the same for this dressing. Makes 24 one-tablespoon servings with 30 calories each.

Carrot Salad

4 cups grated carrots

3 tablespoons lemon juice, freshly squeezed

¼ teaspoon ground mace

¼ cups black currants (dried)

1 green onion, finely-chopped

1 teaspoon brown sugar

¼ teaspoon salt

¼ teaspoon ground nutmeg

Combine all ingredients. Mix well. Let stand for 20 to 30 minutes. Add salad dressing. Makes 6-8 one-half cup servings with 110 calories each.

Walnut Bread

3 cups all-purpose flour
1 cup granulated sugar
4 teaspoons baking powder
1½ teaspoons salt
¼ cup vegetable fat
2 teaspoons orange rind
1½ cups chopped walnuts
1 egg, beaten
1½ cups milk
1 teaspoon vanilla

Preheat oven to 350 degrees. Grease and flour loaf pan. In a bowl, combine flour, sugar, baking powder, and salt. Cut-in vegetable fat until mixture is coarse crumbs. Add orange rind and 1¼ cups of walnuts; in small bowl, combine egg, milk, and vanilla. Add liquid to dry ingredients until blended. Turn into loaf pan. Sprinkle remaining ¼ cup walnuts over top. Bake 60-70 minutes or until toothpick inserted in center comes out clean. Let cool in pan 10 minutes. Turn out on wire rack to cool before slicing. Cut in ½-inch slices. Makes 18 servings of 100 calories each.

Oatmeal Bread

2 cups all-purpose flour
2 teaspoons baking powder
¾ teaspoon soda
1 teaspoon salt
⅓ cup firmly packed brown sugar
1 cup quick-cooking oats, uncooked
1 cup raisins
2 tablespoons molasses
2 tablespoons melted vegetable fat
1¼ cups sour milk or buttermilk

Combine flour, baking powder, soda, salt, and sugar. Crush oats with rolling pin; stir oats and raisins into dry ingredients, mix well. Combine molasses, vegetable fat, and buttermilk; add to flour mixture and stir just to moisten dry ingredients. Pour into greased 9″ × 5″ × 3″ loaf pan. Bake at 350 degrees for 1 hour. Yield: 1 loaf.

Note: one tablespoon plus 2 teaspoons vinegar plus milk will equal 1¼ cups liquid that can be substituted for sour milk. Each one-half inch slice has 95 calories.

Pineapple Muffins

1 cup crushed canned pineapple, drained
½ cup melted vegetable fat
½ cup firmly-packed brown sugar
1 teaspoon salt
1 teaspoon ground cinnamon
¼ teaspoon ground nutmeg
¼ cup chopped nuts
2 cups all-purpose flour
¼ cup sugar
1 tablespoon baking powder
¼ cup milk

Combine pineapple, ¼ cup melted vegetable fat, brown sugar, salt, cinnamon, nutmeg, and nuts. Spoon into 12-muffin pan. Combine flour, sugar, baking powder, milk, and ¼ cup melted vegetable fat. Stir until blended. Spoon mixture in muffin pans. Bake at 425 degrees for 15 to 20 minutes. Turn upside down immediately on tray to remove muffins. Yields 12 muffins with 95 calories each.

Light Rye Bread

1½ cakes compressed yeast or 2 tablespoons active dry yeast
1¹/₃ cups water
3 tablespoons sugar
2 teaspoons salt
4 tablespoons vegetable fat (except coconut oil)
3 cups rye flour
2 cups white flour

Soften yeast in ¹/₃ cup lukewarm water. Add 1 teaspoon sugar. Measure remaining water, salt, sugar and softened fat into a bowl; add dissolved yeast mixture. Pour half of each flour into this liquid mixture and beat until well blended. Add remaining flour; knead on floured board until dough is smooth and will spring back when pressed lightly with finger (about 200 strokes). Place in well-oiled bowl. Let rest until double in bulk (about 1 hour) at 80 degrees. Knead about 100 times and place in two small loaf pans which have been greased only on the bottom. Let rise again until double in bulk (about 30 minutes) at 80 degrees. Bake at 425 degrees for 10 to 15 minutes until brown; then at 350 degrees for 25 to 35 minutes until done. Makes 20 half-inch slices with 90 calories each.

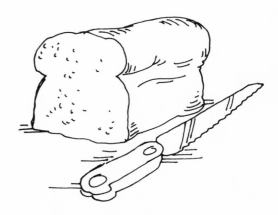

Whole Wheat Biscuits

| ½ cup whole wheat flour |
| 1 cup all-purpose flour |
| 1 teaspoon baking powder |
| ¼ teaspoon soda |
| ½ teaspoon salt |
| ¼ cup vegetable fat |
| ½ to ⅔ cup buttermilk |

Combine flour, baking powder, soda, and salt; cut-in vegetable fat until mixture resembles coarse meal. Add buttermilk and stir until well blended. Turn dough out onto a lightly floured board; knead lightly about 20 seconds. Roll dough to about ½-inch thickness. Cut into round units with a 2-inch biscuit cutter. Place on a greased baking sheet and bake at 450 degrees for 10 to 12 minutes. Makes 12 biscuits with 90 calories each.

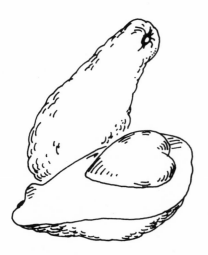

Chocolate Mousse

| 2 tablespoons cold strong coffee |
| 10 oz. bittersweet chocolate, cut in pieces |
| 2 tablespoons brandy |
| 8 eggs, separated |

Combine coffee, chocolate, and brandy in top of double broiler and melt together over heat. Beat egg yolks in a bowl and stir the chocolate mixture into them. Beat well. Set aside to cool.

Beat egg whites in a bowl until stiff and fold into cooled chocolate-egg mixture. Pour into serving dishes and place in cool place for about 4 hours before serving. Makes 8-10 one-half cup servings with 125 calories each. Garnish with whipped cream or nuts.

Minted Fruit Parfait

| 1½ gallon vanilla ice milk |
| 1 tablespoon oil of wintergreen |
| 2 tablespoons lime gelatin |
| 2 pints whipped topping |
| sugar to taste |

Soften the ice milk in a large bowl and beat-in oil of wintergreen. Beat-in 2 tablespoons gelatin. Beat-in whipped topping until stiff and add sugar. Fold in ice cream mixture. Pour in greased mold and cover with aluminum foil. Freeze. Spoon into parfait glasses. Beat remaining whipped topping until stiff and add sugar. Place in frozen mixture and top each serving with fresh mint leaves. Makes 32 one-half cup servings with 50 calories each, (with whipped cream one-half cup has 100 calories.

Apple Sorbet

| 3½ cups sugar |
| 2 cups water |
| 4 cups apple juice |
| 4 cups raw apple, peeled (shred, then toss with lemon juice to preserve freshness) |

Combine sugar and water in heavy 4-quart saucepan. Bring to a boil until syrup thickens, about 5 minutes. Add apple juice and remove from heat. Cool. Add shredded apple and place in ice cream freezer. Freeze as for ice cream. Makes 8 one-half cup servings with 105 calories each.

Angel Food Cake

| 1¼ cups sifted cake flour |
| ½ cup plus ⅓ cups sugar |
| 1½ cups (12) egg whites at room temperature |
| 1¼ teaspoon cream of tartar |
| ¼ teaspoon salt |
| 1 teaspoon vanilla |
| ¼ teaspoon almond extract |

Measure sifted flour. Add ½ cup sugar and sift 4 times. Combine egg whites, cream of tartar, salt, and flavoring in a large bowl. Beat in electric mixer at high speed or with rotary beater until soft peaks form. Add remaining 1⅓ cups of sugar in additions, beating until blended after each addition. Sift-in the flour mixture in 4 additions, folding in with large spoon; turn bowl often. Pour into ungreased 10-inch tube pan. Bake at 375 degrees for 35-40 minutes. Cool cake upside down in a pan on a cake rack, then loosen sides and remove. Each one-inch slice has 60 calories.

Pink-Sunset Parfait Pie

| 1 tablespoon unflavored gelatin |
| ½ cup grapefruit juice, pink |
| 2 cups vanilla ice cream, melted |
| 3 egg whites |
| 1 tablespoon sugar |
| 2 cups pink grapefruit sections |
| 1 baked pastry shell (9-inch) |
| ½ cup whipped cream |

In large saucepan, mix gelatin and grapefruit juice. Let stand for several minutes. Stir over low heat until gelatin is completely dissolved. Remove from heat; stir in ice cream. Chill, stirring occasionally, until mixture mounds slightly when dropped from spoon. In large mixing bowl, beat egg whites until soft peaks form; gradually add sugar and beat until stiff. Fold into gelatin mixture. Fold in grapefruit sections. Turn into prepared crust. Chill until firm. Garnish with whipped cream and additional pink grapefruit sections. Makes 6 1⅓-inch slices with 125 calories each.

Chapter Three

The Stress Prevention Diet: A Three-Meal-a-Day for-a-Lifetime Plan

*T*his three-meal-a-day plan is a lifetime disease prevention diet. It provides a balance of protein, carbohydrate and fat from a variety of fresh foods low in sugar, salt and unsaturated fat that supplies sufficient quantities of nutrients to maintain good health.

Seven Rules for Good Nutrition

In brief, there are seven rules to follow to achieve good nutrition through eating in moderation:

1. Eat a Variety of Foods

You need about 40 different nutrients to stay healthy. These nutrients are in the foods you normally eat.

Most foods contain more than one nutrient but no single food item supplies all the essential nutrients in the amounts that you need.

The greater the variety, the less likely you are to develop either a deficiency or an excess of any single nutrient. Variety also reduces your likelihood of being exposed to excessive amounts of contaminants in any single food item.

2. Maintain Ideal Weight

For most people, their weight should not be more than it was when they were young adults (20 or 25 years old). If you are too fat, your chances of developing some chronic disorders are increased.

It is not well understood why some people can eat much more than others and still maintain normal weight. However, one thing is definite: to lose weight, you must take in fewer calories than your body needs. This means that you must either select foods containing fewer calories or you must increase your activity — or both.

3. Avoid Too Much Fat, Saturated Fat, and Cholesterol

People who live in populations like ours with diets high in saturated fats and cholesterol tend to have high blood cholesterol levels. And usually have greater risks of having heart attacks than people eating low-fat, low-cholesterol diets.

There is controversy about what recommendations are appropriate for healthy Americans. But for the U.S. population as a *whole*, reduction in our current intake of total fat, saturated fat, and cholesterol is sensible. This suggestion is especially appropriate for people who have high blood pressure or who smoke.

4. Eat Foods with Adequate Starch and Fiber

The major sources of energy in the average U.S. diet are carbohydrates and fats.

In trying to reduce your weight to "ideal" levels, carbohydrates have an advantage over fats: carbohydrates contain less than half the number of calories per ounce than fats.

Complex carbohydrate foods are better than *simple* carbohydrates in this regard. Complex carbohydrate foods — such as beans, peas, nuts, seeds, fruits and vegetables, and whole grain breads, cereals, and products — contain many essential nutrients in addition to calories.

Increasing your consumption of certain complex carbohydrates can also help increase dietary fiber.

5. Avoid Too Much Sugar

The major health hazard from eating too much sugar is tooth decay (dental caries). The risk of caries is not simply a matter of how much sugar you eat. The risk increases the more frequently you eat sugar and sweets, especially if you eat between meals, and if you eat foods that stick to the teeth. Watch out for the sugar in the sugar bowl and the sugars and syrups in jams, jellies, candies, cookies, soft drinks, cakes, and pies, as well as sugars found in products such as breakfast cereals, catsup, flavored milks, and ice cream. Frequently, the ingredient label will provide a clue to the amount of sugars in a product.

6. Avoid Too Much Sodium

Table salt contains sodium and chloride — both are essential elements.

Sodium is also present in many beverages and foods that we eat, especially in certain processed foods, condiments, sauces, pickled foods, salty snacks, and sandwich meats. Baking soda, baking powder, monosodium glutamate (MSG), soft drinks, and even medications (many antacids, for instance) contain sodium.

Since most Americans eat more sodium than is needed, consider reducing your sodium intake. Persons, especially if they are obese, who have high blood pressure, should avoid salt. Use less table salt. Eat sparingly those foods to which large amounts of sodium have been added.

7. If You Drink Alcohol, Do So In Moderation

Alcoholic beverages tend to be high in calories and low in other nutrients. Even moderate drinkers may need to drink less if they wish to achieve ideal weight.

One or two drinks daily appear to cause no harm in adults. If you drink you should do so in moderation.

The Foods You Should Eat Everyday

Since this plan is designed as a lifetime pattern for keeping your body stable, it may be helpful to note foods you should include on a daily basis.

CALORIE VALUE ESTIMATE	PATTERN
300-350	6 ounces cooked lean meat
135	3 teaspoons vegetable fat (except coconut oil and palm oil)
90-180	1 to 2 cups nonfat milk
100-440	3 to 4 servings fruit (½ cup average serving)
30-150	2 to 4 vegetables (½ cup average serving)
65-230	2 to 4 slices bread (whole grain)
80	1 egg three times a week as substitute for meat

SHOULD INCLUDE:

Vegetables	Breads	Milk	Meats Poultry	Fats
and	and	and	Fish Dried beans	Sweets
Fruit	Cereals	Cheese	Peas Soybeans Peanuts Peanut Butter	Alcohol (These foods provide calories but few nutrients)

This three-meal-a-day plan includes, for the first time, a special group: *fats, sweets, alcohol.* These foods provide few food nutrients, but plenty of calories. Most of us cannot afford to eat "empty-calorie" foods — foods we may substitute for high quality foods that would provide nutrients needed by the body.

A Daily Plan: Five Basic Food Groups

1. Milk and Cheese Group

SERVINGS:

Adults	2
Children under 9 years old	2-3
Children 9 to 12 years old and Pregnant Women	3
Teens and Nursing Mothers	4

1 serving is:
1 cup milk or yogurt
1¹⁄₃ ounces cheddar or swiss cheese
2 ounces processed cheese food
1½ cups ice cream or ice milk
2 cups cottage cheese

Skim, nonfat, and lowfat milk and milk products provide calcium and keep fat intake down.

2. Meat, Fish, Beans and Poultry Group

½ serving is:
1 to 1½ ounces lean, boneless, cooked meat, poultry, or fish
1 egg
½ to ¾ cup cooked dry beans, peas, lentils, or soybeans
2 tablespoons peanut butter
¼ to ½ cup nuts, sesame or sunflower seeds

Poultry and fish have less fat content than red meats.

3. Bread and Cereal Group

1 serving is:
1 slice bread
½ to ¾ cup cooked cereal or pasta
1 ounce ready-to-eat cereal

Choose whole-grain products often.

4. Vegetable and Fruit Group

1 serving is:
½ cup
A small salad
A medium-sized potato
An orange
½ cantaloupe
½ grapefruit

Have citrus fruit, melon, berries, or tomatoes daily and a dark-green or dark-yellow vegetable frequently. For a good source of fiber, eat unpeeled fruits and vegetables and fruits with edible seeds — berries or grapes.

5. Fats, Sweets and Alcohol Group

These foods provide calories but few nutrients.

It supplies 1500 calories a day. These may be more calories than you need to maintain normal body weight, especially if you are involved in sedentary work.

If the calorie value is too low and your weight is normal, you may add a teaspoon of jelly for breakfast (100 calories) and one slice of a whole grain bread for lunch and dinner (100 calories each).

If you are an active person, the calorie count may be low; if so, add a potato and bread to lunch and dinner. For breakfast, add toast or bread in some form. You will push your total daily calorie intake to between 1800 and 1900 calories.

If you want to lose weight, reduce your calorie content on the diet by 300; eliminate the bread or potato for lunch and dinner and the vegetable fat at breakfast and lunch. If you eliminate the salad dressing for lunch, change your salad to a piece of raw vegetable.

For a bag lunch, include a piece of fruit, a sandwich made of whole wheat bread with special mayonnaise, and milk or fruit juice in a thermos. All are good choices. If you carry a sandwich with two slices of bread, you may need to delete your bread or potato at dinner.

You should not let the calorie value of any diet fall below 1000 unless you are under the care of a physician. A seven-day menu pattern follows, along with its recipes. If you prefer to divide your meal plan into six meals rather than three, simply rearrange the food items, saving some from breakfast for a midmorning snack, some from lunch for your 3:00 P.M. snack, and some from dinner for a bedtime snack. You will not increase the calories unless you add additional foods.

Sample Diet: A Food Pattern to Use as a Guide

(Substitute of food equivalents may be made as desired using the food exchanges on page 114.)

Breakfast

100	½ cup fruit
65	½ cup cereal (or 1 slice whole grain bread)
50	1 teaspoon vegetable fat (except coconut oil or palm oil)
100	½ cup nonfat milk
315	Calories

Lunch

150	3 oz. lean meat (fish, poultry)
100	½ cup potatoes (or macaroni, rice, bread, or crackers)
100	½ cup any vegetable (see exchange list, page 114)
50	½ cup tossed salad (vegetable or fruit)
50	1 teaspoon salad dressing (vegetable fat, except coconut or palm oil)
100	½ cup fruit
100	½ cup nonfat milk
650	Calories

Dinner

150	3 oz. lean meat
100	½ cup potatoes (rice, bread, macaroni, noodles, or crackers)
100	1 cup vegetable salad or fruit salad
50	1 teaspoon vegetable fat (not coconut oil or palm oil)
100	½ cup fruit
100	1 cup nonfat milk
600	Calories
1565	Total Calories

Away-From-Home Meals

The menus in the Stress Prevention Diet are a three-meal-a-day plan. However, any day can be divided into a six-meal plan if you desire.

All the luncheon menus can be adapted to an Away-From-Home Lunch for the office, a meeting or trip. Common sense with regard to spoilage and packaging are all that's necessary: hot soups and cold vegetable or fruit juices should be carried in a thermos. Sandwiches or individual portions of meat (chicken breast) can be wrapped in foil. Salads (fruit, meat, fish, macaroni or green) can be stored in plastic containers with air-tight lids and any dressing can be kept in a separate, small container to keep salad greens fresh up to the time they will be eaten. Milk can be purchased in ½ pint and pint cartons and fresh fruit has its own natural wrapper.

A good lunch could be: tomato bouillon with crackers, cheese pickle spread on rye bread, tossed salad and dressing, fresh fruit and milk.

You may divide your lunch into a mid-morning snack of the bouillon and crackers, and a mid-afternoon snack of fresh fruit. You can have the sandwich and salad as your lunch.

Other lunch suggestions:

1. cream of peanut soup with crackers or toast cubes, fresh spinach salad and dressing, fresh grapes and milk

2. chicken breast, sliced, 1-2 slices bread, green salad and dressing, fresh grapes and milk

3. tomato-corn soup with crackers, cheese toast, stuffed peach and lettuce and milk

By varying combinations and amounts (soup with large salad or sandwich with small salad) and including a fresh fruit and milk you are assuring yourself of a nutritious lunch.

Day One

BREAKFAST
Orange Juice
1 teaspoonful vegetable fat
Whole Wheat Toast
Nonfat Milk

LUNCH
Tomato Bouillon* with crackers
Cheese-Pickle Spread on Rye
Special Tossed Salad*
Deluxe Salad Dressing*
Fruit
Nonfat Milk

DINNER
Chicken a la Lemon Pineapple*
Carrots Marinade*
Green Garden Salad with Buttermilk Dressing*
Sponge Cake*
Fresh Fruit Cup*
Nonfat milk

*Recipes follow

Day Two

BREAKFAST
Orange Wedges
Scrambled Egg
Whole Wheat Toast
Jam
Nonfat milk

LUNCH
Onion Soup* Shrimp in Garlic Sauce*
Rye Toast
Stuffed Meringued Pears*
Green Salad
Nonfat milk

DINNER
Veal Ragout Paris*
Mashed Potatoes
Green Beans and Mushroom Sauce
Cress-Dandelion Salad* with
Special Low-Calorie Dressing*
Nonfat milk

*Recipes Follow

Day Three

BREAKFAST
Baked Stuffed Apple* (Cinnamon,
Brown Sugar, Lemon)
Oatmeal, Nonfat milk
Cheese Wedges
Coffee, Tea

LUNCH
Cream of Peanut Soup* with Toast Cubes
Fresh Spinach Salad*
Low-Sodium French Dressing*
Grapes
Nonfat milk

DINNER
Sweet-Sour Ham*
Baked Tomato
Green Beans Almondine*
Whole Wheat Roll*
Pineapple-Prune Salad
Lemonade

*Recipes follow

Day Four

BREAKFAST
Sliced Bananas
Soft Cooked Egg
Cinnamon Bun
Cocoa

LUNCH
Homemade Tomato-Corn Soup*
Cheese Toast
Stuffed Peaches on Lettuce
Hot Tea with Lemon

DINNER
Lemon-Orange Chicken*
Baked Potato in Skin
Asparagus Tips
Grapefruit-Grape Salad*
Four-Fruit Sherbet*
Nonfat milk

*Recipes Follow

Day Five

BREAKFAST
Cantaloupe
Cream Chipped Beef* on Whole Wheat Toast
Nonfat milk

LUNCH
Chicken-fruit salad* on Whole Wheat
Fruit Dressing*
Tomato-Cucumber*
Spinach-Mushroom Salad*
Italian Dressing*
Hot Lemonade with Orange Slices and Mint

DINNER
Carrot Soup*
Wine-Baked Fish Almondine*
Green Peas
Celery-Lettuce Hearts with Vinegar
Baked Stuffed Apple*
Hot Tea with Lemon

Day Six

BREAKFAST
Sliced Tomatoes
Plain Omelet with Mushrooms*
Boston Brown Bread*
Nonfat milk

LUNCH
Virginia Vegetable Soup* with crackers
Tuna Fish with Egg Slice on Lettuce
Bill's Special Ambrosia*
Nonfat milk

DINNER
Swiss Steak*
Stuffed Eggplant*
Steamed Spinach
Cucumber Marinade (cucumbers in red wine vinegar)
Cherry Jubilee*
Hot Tea with Lemon Slice

*Recipes Follow

*Recipes Follow

Day Seven

BREAKFAST
Orange Juice with Cranberry Juice
Poached Egg on Whole Wheat Toast
Hot Tea with Lemon

DINNER
Stuffed Chicken Breast* with white grape sauce
Steamed Rice
Broccoli with Hollandaise Sauce*
Green Salad with Creamy Cucumber Dressing*
Fruit Cup
Nonfat milk

SUPPER
Cheese Soup*
Fruit Salad Plate (Variety)
(Include gelatin cubes, stuffed dates)
Carrot-Raisin-Pineapple Salad*
Blueberry Muffin*
Lemonade with mint

*Recipes Follow

Special Tossed Salad

¼ head lettuce
4 leaves spinach
4 leaves watercress
1 green pepper
2 stalks celery
2 radishes
1 tomato
1 slice pineapple cubed
lemon slices
bread cubes
2 slices crisp bacon, cooked
salad dressing

Chop lettuce into lettuce-lined bowl. Chop spinach and watercress leaves. Cube green pepper and celery. Mix thoroughly. Slice radishes and place on top. Quarter tomato and dice pineapple for top garnish. Serve with lemon slices, bread cubes, and 2 slices bacon chopped into fine bits. Add your favorite dressing. Makes one serving with 100 calories.

Deluxe Salad Dressing

½ cup tomato juice
2 tablespoons lemon juice or vinegar
1 tablespoon onion, finely chopped
salt and pepper
chopped parsley or green pepper, horseradish or mustard, etc. may be added if desired

Combine ingredients in a jar with a tightly fitted top. Shake well before using. Makes 16 one-tablespoon servings with 15 calories each.

Tomato Bouillon

2 tablespoons vegetable (except coconut oil)
¾ cup chopped onions
6 cups tomato juice
1 bay leaf
½ teaspoon dried oregano leaves
¼ teaspoon seasoned salt
⅛ teaspoon pepper
½ cup chopped celery with leaves

In hot fat in medium saucepan, sauté onion, stirring, until golden (about 3 minutes). Add other ingredients. Simer 15 minutes. Stir occasionally. Strain. Taste for seasoning. Serve hot or cold. Makes 6 one cup servings with 90 calories each.

Sponge Cake

⅓ cup sugar
⅓ cup flour
pinch salt
3 eggs
½ tablespoon lemon juice
¼ teaspoon grated rind of 1 lemon

Sift sugar, flour, and salt together. Separate egg whites from yolks and place whites in large bowl. Beat yolks with lemon juice and rind. With a rotary beater, beat egg whites until they peak but are not dry. Alternately fold in the flour and egg yolk mixtures. Pour into ungreased loaf pan 8½″ × 4½″ × 2½″. Bake in a slow oven (325 degrees) for about an hour. Invert on wire rack and allow to cool. Remove from pan by running the blade of a spatula around the edge. Makes 12 one-inch servings with 60 calories each.

Chicken a la Lemon-Pineapple

1 (3 pound broiler/fryer) up
¼ tablespoon sage
½ teaspoon salt
1½ cups bread crumbs
2 teaspoons dried rosemary leaves
1 teaspoon ginger
1 tablespoon orange peel
1 tablespoon vegetable fat melted (except coconut oil)
¼ cup drained crushed pineapple
¼ cup pineapple juice
½ cup water
¼ cup finely-chopped celery
1 teaspoons lemon juice (fresh)

Remove skin from chicken. Rinse chicken with cold water and drain. Dry inside and outside. Rub cavity of each chicken piece with sage and salt. Combine bread crumbs, rosemary, ginger, celery, orange peel, and fat in bowl. Toss lightly. Place pieces of chicken in baking dish. Add crushed pineapple, orange juice, lemon and pineapple juice over the chicken. Add water and place in oven. Bake at 375 degrees about 1 hour or until chicken is tender. Makes 5-6 4-ounce servings with 135 calories each.

Buttermilk Dressing

1 cup buttermilk
½ teaspoon onion juice
¼ teaspoon salt
1¼ tablespoons lemon juice

Combine all ingredients in jar with tight-fitting lid. Shake vigorously to blend. Store in refrigerator until ready to use. Shake just before using. Makes 16 one-tablespoon servings with 25 calories each.

Fresh Fruit Cup

| ½ pineapple |
| 3 well-ripened bananas |
| 3 oranges |
| 1 cup strawberries |
| 2 tablespoons lemon juice |
| sugar |

Peel and dice the pineapple, bananas, and oranges. Wash and hull strawberries. Mix all together, with the lemon juice and sugar, and set in the refrigerator until cold.

Peel and slice 3 oranges and arrange in a glass dish alternate layers of oranges and sugar until all the fruit is used. Whip some sweet cream to very stiff peaks. Sweeten and flavor it and spread it over the oranges. Serve very cold. Makes 6 one-half cup servings with 100 calories each.

Carrots Marinade

| 1 cup white vinegar |
| ¼ cup chopped onion |
| 1 teaspoon salt |
| 1 teaspoon mixed pickling spices |
| 9 carrots quartered lengthwise (½ pound) |

In medium saucepan, heat vinegar, onion, salt, and pickling spice to boiling. Add carrots, bring to boiling. Reduce heat; simmer, covered, 5 minutes. Pour into shallow baking dish. Let cool Refrigerate 2 hours. Drain just before serving. Makes 6 one-half cup servings with 100 calories each.

Onion Soup

| 4 medium onions |
| 3 tablespoons celery, chopped |
| 2 tablespoons vegetable fat (except coconut oil) |
| 2 tablespoons flour |
| 1 teaspoon salt |
| ⅛ teaspoon pepper |
| 2 cups hot chicken stock |
| 2 cups hot nonfat milk |
| 1 tablespoon parsley chopped |

Cook onions and celery until tender. Drain and sieve. Melt fat, add flour and seasoning, then stock and milk, stirring constantly. Cook until smooth, about 5 minutes. Add onions, celery and parsley. Beat with egg beater until smooth. Makes one-cup servings with 100 calories each.

Shrimp in Garlic Sauce

| 2 tablespoons vegetable oil (except coconut oil) |
| 2 pounds uncooked, deveined shrimp |
| 2 small cloves garlic, finely chopped |
| ¼ cup tomato paste |
| 2 teaspoons salt |
| ½ teaspoon pepper |
| ½ teaspoon dried basil leaves |
| 1 cup chopped onion |

In hot oil in large skillet, over medium heat, sauté shrimp, turning several times about 5 minutes, or just until they turn pink. Remove from heat. Stir in other ingredients along with 1 cup water. Simmer, covered, until heated through. Makes 6 4-ounce servings with 150 calories each.

Veal Ragout Paris

1 tablespoon vegetable oil (except coconut oil)

1½ pound veal shoulder, cut into 2-inch cubes

1 clove garlic, finely chopped

1 tablespoon flour

1½ teaspoon salt

½ teaspoon pepper

1½ cups boiling water

1½ cups sliced carrots

1 cup sliced celery

2 medium potatoes pared and quartered

1½ cup peas

½ teaspoon dried marjoram leaves

In hot fat in Dutch oven or heavy skillet, brown veal well on all sides (in several batches, if necessary). Add garlic. Sauté 3 minutes. Sprinkle flour, salt, and pepper over veal. Gradually stir in boiling water. Reduce heat. Simmer, covered, 1 hour, stirring occasionally. Add carrots, celery, potatoes, peas, and marjoram. Simmer, covered, about 25 minutes or until vegetables are tender. (If mixture seems dry, add a small amount of boiling water.) Makes 6 4-ounce servings with 145 calories each.

Cress-Dandelion Salad

1 cup dandelion greens

1 cup watercress

8 thin slices raw onion

French dressing

The dandelion should be fresh and young. Wash the leaves carefully and drain well. Arrange them in a salad bowl with the cress. Add the slices of onion and pour the French dressing over all. Makes 2 one-half cup servings with 50 calories each.

Stuffed Meringued Pears

6 large pears

6 tablespoons sugar

grated lemon rind

candied ginger

3 egg whites

¼ cup powdered sugar

Pare and core the pears. Place them in a baking dish and fill the center of each with one tablespoon sugar and a little grated lemon rind or candied ginger. Add three or four tablespoons water and bake until tender. Cover them with a meringue made with stiffly beaten egg whites and the sugar. Brown quickly. Makes 6 servings with 95 calories each.

Special Low Calorie Dressing

½ teaspoon gelatin
1 tablespoon water
¼ cup boiling water
½ teaspoon prepared mustard
½ teaspoon sweet pickle juice
1 teaspoon salt
1 teaspoon grated lemon rind
½ cup lemon juice
¼ teaspoon onion juice
¼ teaspoon paprika
⅛ teaspoon curry powder
1 pinch black pepper
1 pinch cayenne pepper

In a half-pint jar, soften gelatin in tablespoon of water. Add remaining ingredients and stir until dissolved. Shake well. Chill. Makes 16 one-tablespoon servings with 30 calories each.

Baked Stuffed Apples

6 large tart apples
1 cup chopped bananas
1 cup chopped cranberries
lemon wedge
1 cup brown sugar
1 teaspoon cinnamon
chopped nut meats

Cut off the stem ends of the apples, but do not peel them. Remove all the core and part of the pulp, leaving the walls of the cup about three-fourths inch thick. Mix bananas, cranberries, sugar, and cinnamon. Fill the cavities in the apples with this mixture; cover with chopped nutmeats. Serve with lemon wedge. Bake in oven at 425 degrees for about 30 minutes. Makes 6 servings of 175 calories each.

Green Beans Almondine

2 pounds fresh green beans
½ cup minced onion + ⅓ cup for sauté
1 cup water
⅓ cup slivered almonds
3 tablespoons melted vegetable fat (except coconut oil)

Remove strings from green beans; cut beans into 1½ pieces and wash thoroughly. Place in a 5-quart Dutch oven with onions. Add water. Bring to a boil, then reduce heat. Cover and simmer for 1 hour. Drain-off excess liquid (save for soup). Sauté onion and almonds in oil until onion is tender. Add to beans, along with salt; toss lightly. Makes 8 one-half cup servings with 110 calories each.

Low-Sodium French Dressing

¼ cup vegetable oil, low-sodium (except coconut oil)
¼ cup cider vinegar
½ cup water
2 teaspoons sugar
1 teaspoon dry mustard
½ teaspoon paprika
dash pepper

Combine all ingredients; heat well with rotary beater or shake well in jar with tight-fitting cover. Makes 16 one-tablespoon servings with 15 calories each.

Cream of Peanut Soup

(A specialty of the Hotel Roanoke, Roanoke, Virginia. Their recipe is a secret; this recipe comes nearest to it.)

½ cup vegetable fat (except coconut oil)
1 cup thinly-sliced celery
¼ cup minced green onions
2 teaspoons flour
2 cups chicken stock or broth
½ cup creamy peanut butter
1½ cups light cream
6 tablespoons crushed peanuts

Melt fat in large saucepan over low heat and add celery and onion. Cook until tender but not browned. Add flour and stir until mixture is smooth. Gradually add chicken broth and bring to a boil. Blend in peanut butter and simmer about 15 minutes. Stir in cream just before serving. Add crushed peanuts to the top of each serving. Makes 6 one-cup servings with 135 calories each.

Sweet-Sour Ham

1⅛ cups pineapple tidbits, drained
½ cup pineapple syrup
1 cup green pepper, cut in ¼ inch pieces
½ cup water chestnuts, sliced
1 tablespoon sugar
1 tablespoon cornstarch
1 teaspoon soy sauce
1 tablespoon vinegar
½ cup chicken broth (or chicken bouillon)
½ teaspoon salt
dash pepper
1 cup lean diced ham

Cook pineapple in lightly greased skillet for 5 minutes. Add pineapple syrup, green pepper, and water chestnuts. Cover and simmer for 10 minutes. Combine sugar, cornstarch, soy sauce, vinegar, chicken broth, and seasonings. Add to pineapple. Cook, stirring constantly, until thickened. Add ham. Heat through thoroughly. Serve over boiled rice. Makes 6 4-ounce servings with 115 calories each.

Fresh Spinach Salad

1 pint spinach
2 hard-cooked eggs
low-sodium French Dressing

Wash spinach carefully. Select only thick, tender leaves (save others and stems for cooking). If too large, tear to size. Shake off excess water. Chop whites and yolks of eggs separately and turn into bowl with leaves. Moisten with tart French dressing. Any mild-flavored vegetable may be added for variation. Makes 2 one-half cup servings with 60 calories each.

Whole Wheat Rolls

2 pkgs. dry yeast

2 cups warm milk (105 degrees to 115 degrees)

1 egg

⅓ cup sugar

1 teaspoon salt

3½ cups whole wheat flour

1 cup vegetable fat (except coconut oil)

3 to 3½ cups all-purpose flour

3 tablespoons vegetable fat (for greasing bowl and pans)

Dissolve yeast in milk in a large bowl. Stir in egg, sugar, and salt. Add whole wheat flour and vegetable fat, mixing well. Gradually add enough all-purpose flour to form a moderately stiff dough, beating well after each addition.

Place dough in a lightly greased bowl, turning to grease top. Cover and let rise in a warm place (85 degrees) free from drafts, for 1½ hours or until doubled in bulk. Punch down; cover and let rise 30 minutes or until dough is doubled in bulk.

Lightly grease muffin pans. Shape dough into 1-inch balls; place 3 balls in each muffin cup. Brush tops with melted vegetable fat. Cover and let rise 45 minutes or until doubled in bulk. Bake at 400 degrees for 12 to 15 minutes or until golden brown. Yield: about 4 dozen rolls with 90 calories each.

Tomato-Corn Soup

1 cup nonfat milk (dry)

4 cups water

1 cup tomato soup (condensed)

½ cup cream-style corn

¼ teaspoon curry powder

Add water to milk and mix thoroughly.

Add milk gradually to the tomato soup. Stir in the corn. Sprinkle the curry powder on top and heat over low heat until very hot. Makes 5 one cup servings with 110 calories each.

Orange-Lemon Baked Chicken

1 frying chicken (2½-3 lbs.) cut in serving pieces

3 tablespoons vegetable oil (except coconut oil)

3 tablespoons fresh lemon juice

1 crushed clove garlic

1½ teaspoon salt

dash pepper

chopped parsley

1 cup fresh orange sections

Arrange chicken in shallow casserole or baking dish. Mix all other ingredients and pour over chicken. Cover and bake at 350 degrees until tender, about 45 to 50 minutes. Uncover casserole the last 10 minutes to allow chicken to brown. Before serving, sprinkle with chopped parsley. Makes 4 4-ounce servings with 135 calories each.

Four-Fruit Sherbet

2 cups mashed bananas (3 medium bananas)

1/3 cup sugar

1/8 teaspoon salt

1/2 cup corn syrup

1/4 cup cranberry juice

1/4 cup lemon juice

1/3 cup orange juice

1 cup nonfat milk

1 egg white

To mashed bananas, add sugar, salt, and corn syrup. Mix thoroughly. Add cranberry, lemon, and orange juices. Add milk gradually. Stir constantly. Beat egg white until peaks are formed. Fold into fruit mixture. Place in shallow pan or a freezer tray and freeze. Makes 2 one-half cup servings with 145 calories each.

Grapefruit and Grape Salad

2 cups grapefruit sections

1/2 cup Malaga grapes, peeled and seeded

2 tablespoons grape juice

2 tablespoons French dressing

Peel fine large grapefruit and separate the sections, removing every particle of the bitter white inner skin. Peel and seed the grapes and mix with the grapefruit. Set, uncovered, in refrigerator until very cold. Pour over them the grape juice and French dressing. Makes 4 one-half cup servings with 120 calories each.

Creamed Chipped Beef

1/4 cup vegetable fat (except coconut oil)

1/4 lb. dried beef

1 cup finely diced celery

3 tablespoons flour

2 cups milk, nonfat

2 baked potatoes or 2 cups mashed potatoes

Melt fat in large skillet. Cut beef in small pieces with a scissors and add to fat with the celery. Sauté for about 7 minutes or until beef is lightly browned. Sprinkle flour over beef mixture and stir until flour is blended smoothly with the fat. Add the milk gradually. Stir to keep smooth and cook over low heat until mixture bubbles and thickens. Serve hot over potatoes or toast, bite-sized shredded wheat biscuits or noodles. Makes 4 one-half cup servings with 140 calories each.

NOTE: Celery may be omitted.

Chicken-Fruit Salad

2 cups pineapple chunks

1 apple, cored and sliced

1 cup seedless grapes

3 cups diced cooked chicken

1/3 cup toasted slivered almonds

lettuce

whipped Cream Fruit Dressing

Drain pineapple chunks, reserving juice. Dip apple slices in pineapple juice. Combine fruit and chicken, chill. Add Whipped Cream Fruit Dressing and toss lightly. Serve on lettuce and top with almonds. Makes 4 one-half cup servings of 130 calories each.

Fruit Dressing

3 tablespoons vegetable fat (except coconut oil)
3 tablespoons all-purpose flour
¼ cup sugar
1 teaspoon salt
⅓ cup lemon juice
⅓ cup pineapple juice
2 egg yolks, slightly beaten
½ cup whipped cream

Melt fat in a small saucepan over low heat; blend in flour. Add sugar, salt, lemon juice and pineapple juice; cook until thickened, stirring constantly. Stir a small amount of hot mixture into egg yolks; stir into remaining hot mixture. Cook about 2 minutes, stirring constantly. Chill. Fold in whipped cream. Makes 8 one tablespoon servings with 35 calories each.

Tomato, Cucumber, Spinach and Mushroom Salad

1 pound fresh spinach, torn
6 slices bacon, cooked and crumbled
6 cucumber wedges
⅔ cup sliced fresh mushrooms
½ cup tomatoes, fresh, diced

Combine spinach, mushrooms, bacon and tomatoes in large salad bowl. Toss lightly. Serve on salad plates with cucumber wedges on each. Add special Italian dressing over each serving. Makes 6 one-half cup servings with 125 calories each.

Italian Dressing

¼ cup olive oil
1 tablespoon lemon rind, grated
1 clove garlic, minced
1 tablespoon Parmesan cheese, grated
2 tablespoons lemon juice
dash salt
½ teaspoon oregano or thyme

Combine all ingredients, mix well, shake before using. Store in covered jar or bottle. Makes 8 one table-spoon servings with 25 calories each.

Wine-Baked Fish Almondine

2 lbs. fish fillets, fresh or frozen
3 medium-sized fresh tomatoes finely cut or 1 cup canned tomatoes
1 onion, chopped
1 green pepper, chopped
salt and pepper
½ cup dry sherry
1 cup almonds, slivered

Place fish in a baking dish. Cover with tomatoes, onion, green pepper, salt, pepper, and sherry wine. Bake uncovered in a moderate oven (350 degrees) about 20 minutes or until fish is tender. Add almonds and allow to brown, about 10 minutes. Makes 6 4-ounce servings with 140 calories each.

Carrot Soup

3 tablespoons vegetable oil (except coconut oil)
6 carrots, peeled and sliced
2 medium onions, finely chopped
1 cup chopped celery
¼ cup all-purpose flour
2 tablespoons cornstarch
2 quarts chicken broth
¼ teaspoon salt
¼ teaspoon pepper
½ cup diced processed cheese spread

Melt vegetable oil in large Dutch oven. Add carrots, onions, and celery. Sauté until onion is tender.

Stir flour and cornstarch into vegetable mixture. Cook over low heat 1 minute, stirring constantly. Gradually stir in chicken broth, salt, and pepper. Simmer over medium heat about 8 minutes or until the carrots are crisp-tender, stirring occasionally. Reduce heat to low. Add cheese to soup, stirring until melted. Makes 10 one-cup servings with 145 calories each.

Baked Stuffed Apple

See Recipes: Day Three, Chapter Three

Boston Brown Bread

1 cup cornmeal
1 cup whole rye flour
1 cup whole wheat flour
½ teaspoon soda
1 teaspoon baking powder
1 teaspoon salt
¾ cup molasses
2 cups buttermilk
2 tablespoons vegetable fat (except coconut oil), melted
1 cup raisins, washed and dried

Stir cornmeal, rye flour, and whole wheat flour with a spoon to fluff them up before measuring. Lift lightly into a cup with a spoon to measure. Sift cornmeal, rye, and whole wheat flour with the soda, baking powder, and salt 3 times. Add the bran from rye and wheat that would not go through sifter. Combine molasses, buttermilk, and fat. Add to dry ingredients and stir until thoroughly mixed. Stir in raisins. Spoon batter into 3 well-greased molds, filling them about ⅔ full. Cover with lids or double thickness of waxed paper. Steam 1½ hours or until springy when pressed and no longer sticky. Cool a few minutes, then remove bread from molds. Serve warm. (Improvise a steamer by placing a rack on the bottom of a deep kettle. Cover the bottom with boiling water and place molds on rack. Cover tightly. Add more boiling water as water boils away. Steam until firm to touch.) A half-inch slice has 95 calories.

NOTE: One pound baking powder cans make very fine molds for the bread. Small slice will substitute for 1 serving of any other bread.

Swiss Steak

2 lbs. round steak
garlic cloves
flour
1 teaspoon salt
⅛ teaspoon pepper
½ cup chopped onion
2 cups tomatoes heated to boiling

Wipe the steak with a damp cloth and trim the fat off the edges. Rub it with a half clove of garlic. With the edge of a heavy plate pound into both sides as much flour, combined with the salt and pepper, as the steak will hold. Cut the steak into pieces or leave it whole. Pan-brown in a seasoned or salted skillet to prevent it from sticking. Pour off all drippings. Place steak in casserole. Add the chopped onions and tomatoes. Cover casserole closely and place in a slow oven (275 degrees) for 2 hours or more. Remove steak to a hot plate. Makes 6 4-ounce servings with 135 calories each.

Plain Omelet With Mushrooms

2 eggs
¼ teaspoon salt
dash pepper
¼ cup sliced mushrooms
2 tablespoons water
1 tablespoon vegetable fat (except coconut oil)

Beat eggs until well blended. Add seasonings and water. Melt fat in small frying pan; add egg mixture and sliced mushrooms. Place over medium heat and lift edges of omelet as it cooks. Tip frying pan to allow liquid to run under the firm portion. Shake over heat until slightly brown and fold with spatula from handle of frying pan to outer edge. Slip onto a hot plate and garnish with parsley. Makes 1 serving with 140 calories.

Virginia Vegetable Soup

½ cup mixed vegetables: carrots, peas, corn
½ small onion, chopped
2 potatoes cooked, diced
½ cup cabbage, shredded
1 stalk celery, diced
¼ cup tomato juice, or
½ cup canned tomatoes
1 cup meat stock or bouillon cubes and 1 cup water

Prepare vegetables and add to broth. Boil together until vegetables are just tender, about 20 minutes. Makes 1-2 one-cup servings with 100 calories each.

Stuffed Eggplant

1 large eggplant, about 1½ pounds
½ cup water
¼ cup chopped onion
1 tablespoon vegetable oil
1½ cup cream of mushroom soup
1 tablespoon chopped parsley
½ teaspoon Worcestershire sauce
1 cup finely-crushed crackers

Slice off one end of eggplant. Remove pulp to within ½ inch of skin. Cook eggplant pulp in a small amount of boiling water until tender, about 10 minutes. Drain thoroughly. Cook onion in fat until tender but not brown. Add soup, eggplant pulp, parsley, Worcestershire sauce, and all of the cracker crumbs except 2 tablespoons. Fill eggplant shell with mixture. Place in 10″ × 6″ × 2″ baking dish. Sprinkle reserved crumbs on top. Carefully pour hot water in bottom of dish to depth of one-half inch. Bake at 375 degrees until heated through, 50 to 60 minutes. Makes 4-6 one-half cup servings with 125 calories each.

Cherries Jubilee (Salad or Dessert)

2 cups pitted, dark, sweet cherries, halved
⅓ cup sherry-flavored gelatin
½ cup cream sherry
3 oz. cream cheese, cut in small cubes
½ cup chopped pecans
Lettuce leaves
8 pear halves, cooked and drained

Drain cherries, reserving syrup. Add water to syrup to make 1½ cups liquid. In medium saucepan, combine gelatin and syrup mixture. Heat and stir until gelatin dissolves. Remove from heat. Stir in sherry. Chill until partially set. Reserve 2 pear halves; slice and set aside for garnish. Chop remaining pears; fold into gelatin along with cherries, cheese, and pecans. Turn into 4½ cup mold. Chill until firm. Unmold, garnish with lettuce leaves and pear slices. Makes 8 one-half cup servings with 130 calories each.

Bill's Special Ambrosia

See Recipes: Day Six, Chapter Two

Recipes: Day Seven

White Grape Sauce

3 tablespoons vegetable fat (except coconut oil)
3 tablespoons all-purpose flour
1½ cups chicken broth
2 tablespoons sugar
½ teaspoon salt
2 teaspoons lemon juice
2 cups white grapes, drained

Melt vegetable fat in a heavy saucepan over low heat; add flour, stirring constantly until smooth. Cook 1 minute, stirring constantly. Gradually add broth, cook over medium heat, stirring constantly until thickened and bubbly. Stir in sugar, salt, and lemon juice. Add grapes just before serving. Makes 2½ cups with 200 calories each.

Hollandaise Sauce

¼ cup vegetable fat (except coconut oil)
2 egg yolks, slightly beaten
¼ cup melted vegetable fat (except coconut oil)
1 tablespoon lemon juice
pinch of salt
dash of cayenne

Combine ¼ cup vegetable fat and egg yolks in top of a double boiler. Place over hot water (do not let water boil). Beat constantly with a whisk until fat melts. Gradually add ¼ cup melted fat, beating well. Add lemon juice and salt, beating well. Cook, beating constantly, until mixture thickens. Remove from heat and stir in cayenne. Serve immediately. Makes 6 one-tablespoon servings with 35 calories each.

Broccoli With Hollandaise Sauce

1 2-lb. bunch fresh broccoli
Hollandaise Sauce (recipe follows)

Trim off large leaves of broccoli. Remove tough ends of lower stalks and wash broccoli thoroughly. If stalks are more than 1 inch in diameter, make lengthwise slits in stalks.

Cook broccoli in a small amount of boiling salted water 15 to 20 minutes or until tender. Drain well, serve with Hollandaise Sauce. Makes 4-5 one-half cup servings with 130 calories each.

Blueberry Buttermilk Muffins

2 cups all-purpose flour
½ cup sugar
2¼ teaspoons baking powder
1 teaspoon salt
½ teaspoon soda
1 egg, slightly beaten
1 cup buttermilk
¼ cup melted vegetable fat (except coconut oil)
1 cup blueberries

Combine dry ingredients in a mixing bowl; set aside. Combine egg, buttermilk and fat; mix well. Make a well in center of dry ingredients, pour in liquid ingredients. Stir just until moistened. Fold in blueberries.

Fill greased muffin pan two-thirds full. Bake at 425 degrees for 20 to 25 minutes. Remove from pan immediately. Makes 18 muffins with 100 calories each.

Carrot-Raisin Pineapple Salad

1 cup grated raw carrot
1 cup shredded cabbage
¼ cup seedless raisins
1 cup crushed pineapple (drained)
½ teaspoon salt
2 tablespoons lemon juice
¼ cup mayonnaise or cooked salad dressing*

Lightly toss carrot, cabbage, raisins, pineapple, salt, and lemon juice until well combined. Refrigerate until ready to serve. Just before serving, toss with mayonnaise (special). Makes 4 one-half cup servings with 125 calories each.

*See recipe

Stuffed Chicken Breasts With White Grape Sauce

6 whole chicken breasts, skinned and boned
6 slices white bread cut into ¼-inch cubes
¼ cup minced onion
¼ cup finely chopped celery
½ cup melted vegetable fat (except coconut oil)
¼ teaspoon salt
1 teaspoon pepper
1 teaspoon rubbed sage
½ (6 oz.) package frozen crabmeat, thawed, undrained and flaked
½ cup all-purpose flour
¼ cup melted vegetable fat
White Grape Sauce*

Place each chicken breast on a sheet of waxed paper, flatten to ¼ inch thickness, using a meat mallet or rolling pin.

Combine next 8 ingredients, stirring well. Spoon stuffing into center of each chicken breast. Fold long sides of chicken over stuffing, fold ends over and secure with toothpicks.

Dredge each chicken breast in flour. Brown chicken on all sides in ¼ cup melted fat. Transfer chicken to a 15″ × 10″ × 1″ jelly-roll pan. Bake at 375 degrees for 25 minutes or until tender. Serve with White Grape Sauce. Garnish with orange slices. Makes 6 4-ounce servings with 160 calories each.

*See Recipe p. 81

Chapter Four
Personal Programs for Handling Stress

The Tea Prescription

*T*o gather some individual facts about how others relieve stress, I questioned one hundred professional dietitians and nutritionists. Aware of the needs of others but, at the same time, managing stress in their own lives, these professionals shared with me their ideas on stress prevention.

Their ideas sprang from their experiences as health experts across the United States, working in colleges and universities, medical centers, hospitals, rehabilitation centers, public health centers, and as self-employed practitioners who instruct and counsel patients daily.

Their answers were not surprising. Many nutritionists, for example, agree that tea of all kinds, drunk hot down to the last drop, is a wonderful stress reliever.

The English credit tea for their ability to promote well-being, prevent argument and provide compromise. They say, "tea neither promotes nor stimulates ill will." We Americans have never given tea the same credit, even though early Americans created and developed much good will at the teatable.

Tea served chilled or steaming contains zero calories the same as coffee. Each of these beverages contains caffeine. However, tea contains 60 to 75 milligrams of caffeine compared to 250 milligrams of caffeine in the same amount of coffee. Teas from China have a lower caffeine content than teas from other countries. And some teas are caffeine free.

The Chineese have watched Americans drink tea and wondered about our practice of heating tea to make it hot then adding ice in it to make it cold and adding sugar to make it sweet then putting in lemon to make it sour. The tea recipes that follow include additions which provide nutritional value while at the same time decreasing the caffeine content per serving. The flavor of tea combines well with high nutritional beverages such as orange and lemon juices.

Yes, the additions of foods to tea recipes will add total calories. The following table shows how many:

8 ounces	calories
Coffee (black)	0
Ginger ale	80
Cola	88
Club Soda	0
Apple juice	106
Lemonade	89*
Grapefruit juice (no sugar added)	54*
Orange juice (no sugar added)	80*
Grape juice (no sugar added)	120*
Tea	0
Pineapple juice (no sugar added)	126*
Lemon juice (one tablespoon)	4*
Vegetable juice (six ounces)	28*
Wine (red or white; four ounces)	100

*Note: These have nutritional value other than carbohydrates.

Some of the nutritionists favorite recipes follow:

Spiced Tea Marie

4 cups boiling water
8 tea bags
4 cups apple juice
1 teaspoon ground allspice
½ cup brown sugar
6 cinnamon sticks
8 orange slices, halved
12 whole cloves

Pour boiling water over teabags. Cover and allow to steep about 10 minutes. Remove teabags. Heat apple juice, ground allspice, and brown sugar in saucepan and let simmer about 5 minutes. Combine with hot tea. Stir. Add orange slices and cloves. Serve in heated cups or mugs. Add ½ cinnamon stick to each serving. Makes 12 one-cup servings with 75 calories each.

Ginger Tea

1 teaspoon instant tea
2 tablespoons water
ice cubes
¾ cup ginger ale, chilled

Place tea in glass. Add water. Stir to dissolve. Add ice cubes. Pour in ginger ale. Stir. Makes one serving of 100 calories.

Tea Topaz

4 cups water
6 teabags
1 cinnamon stick
½ teaspoon whole cloves
½ teaspoon ground ginger
3 tablespoons sugar

Bring water to boil. Rinse teapot with hot water to warm. Place teabags, cinnamon stick, cloves, and ginger in teapot. Pour boiling water over spices. Add sugar. Stir. Pour tea into cups. If more tea is desired, add additional hot water. Makes five one-cup servings with 20 calories each.

Trim-Down Tea

3 cups vegetable juice (V-8)
1 cup tea, brewed
⅛ teaspoon cinnamon
3 orange slices, cut in half

Place juice, tea, and cinnamon in saucepan. Heat. Stir. Serve in cups or mugs. Garnish each with ½ orange slice. Makes 6 one-cup servings with 100 calories each.

Cranberry Tea

4 cups water
12 cloves, whole
2 cinnamon sticks
2 tablespoons sugar
4 tea bags
2 cups cranberry juice

Place water, cloves, cinnamon sticks, and sugar in saucepan. Cover and bring to boil. Remove cinnamon sticks. Remove mixture from heat. Place teabags in mixture. Cover and allow to steep for five minutes or until tea is as strong as desired. Remove teabags. Add cranberry juice. Stir. Place over heat until steam rices — do not allow to boil. Serve in cups or mugs. Makes 6 one-cup servings with 70 calories each.

Tea Julep

4 cups cold water
15 tea bags
½ cup sugar
4 cups hot water
1½ cups frozen concentrate lemonade
¼ cup lime juice
2 teaspoons rum flavoring
fresh mint leaves
ice

Bring 4 cups water to boil. Remove from heat. Add tea bags. Allow to steep for 10 to 15 minutes; remove tea bags. Dissolve sugar in hot tea. Strain into pitcher. Add 4 cups cold water, frozen lemonade, lime juice, and flavoring. Pour into glasses of ice. Garnish with mint leaves. Makes 14 one-cup servings with 60 calories each.

Hot Spiced Tea

¾ cup honey
1 teaspoon ginger
4 tablespoons instant tea
2 quarts boiling water
½ cup lemon juice
1 cinnamon stick per serving

Mix honey, ginger, and instant tea in container. Stir in boiling water. Last add lemon juice and stir. Serve in cups or mugs. Add 1 cinnamon stick to each serving. Makes 10-12 one-cup servings of 70 calories each.

The Soup Solution

Nutritionists believe that you should eat in moderation. Moderation means eating light or low calorie foods. Eating light is especially necessary when the body is under stress. If the stress is acute, you may be best off if you eat only a bowl of soup which can be soothing and, at the same time, nourishing.

Here are some soups nutritionists enjoy as stress relievers. Serve them piping hot to spoon from bowls or sip from mugs — slowly.

Watercress-Potato Soup

1 tablespoon vegetable fat
½ cup chopped celery
½ cup chopped leek or onion
3 medium potatoes, diced
3½ cups chicken broth (see recipe p. 45)
1¾ cups chopped watercress
¼ teaspoon salt
1½ tablespoons fresh lemon juice
½ cup whipping cream

In casserole dish, heat vegetable fat until melted. Stir in celery, leeks or onion and cook uncovered about 3 minutes. Stir. Stir in potatoes, chicken broth, watercress (leaving ¼ cup) and salt. Cover and cook until simmering. Stir and cook for about 5 minutes. Add lemon juice. Pureé in blender. Return soup to casserole and stir in cream. Allow to cook until simmering. Garnish with fresh watercress (¼ cup). Makes 6 one-cup servings with 150 calories each.

Quick Shrimp Soup

1½ cups chicken broth (see recipe p. 45)
1¼ cups condensed green pea soup
1¼ cups condensed tomato soup
1 cup chopped raw shrimp
¼ cup sherry
¼ teaspoon salt
1 cup whipping cream, whipped
1 tablespoon chopped chives or parsley

Combine chicken broth and soups in casserole dish. Cook about 4 minutes, stirring until simmering. Stir in shrimp. Cook until shrimp turns pink. Stir in sherry and salt. Fold in whipped whipping cream. Garnish with chives or parsley. Makes 6 one-cup servings with 150 calories each.

Lemon Soup

6 cups chicken broth (see recipe p. 45)
¼ cup cooked rice
3 eggs, room temperature
¼ cup fresh lemon juice, room temperature
¼ teaspoon salt

Heat to simmer chicken broth in casserole dish for about 12 minutes. Stir in rice and cook. Stir. Allow rice to become tender. Beat eggs in bowl. Add lemon juice gradually and stir. Heat broth to simmer. Stir in egg and lemon juice. Cover. Allow to simmer about 5 minutes. The egg should be set, floating golden shreds. Add salt. Serve hot. Makes 6 one-cup servings with 100 calories each.

Cream of Mushroom Soup

½ ounce imported dried mushrooms
1 cup boiling water
½ cup vegetable fat
½ cup diced onion
1½ pounds fresh mushrooms, sliced
3 tablespoons flour
2 tablespoons chicken stock
7 cups water
1 tablespoon lemon juice
1 tablespoon salt
2 cups light cream
1 cup sour cream
3 tablespoons chopped parsley

Wash dried mushrooms. Place in bowl. Cover with boiling water (1 cup). Soak for 30 minutes. Melt vegetable fat in saucepan. Add onion. Sauté until onion is transparent. Add half of fresh mushrooms and sauté until all liquid has evaporated. Add flour, stir and cook for about 5 minutes. Dissolve chicken base in cold water. Add to saucepan. Stir until smooth. Add remaining fresh mushrooms. Add soaked dried mushrooms and liquid, lemon juice and salt. Bring to simmer. Cook slowly for about 15 minutes. Add light cream, sour cream and parsley. Simmer for about 15 minutes. Garnish with parsley. Makes 12 one-cup servings with 175 calories each.

The Fruit Solution

Many nutritionists suggest substituting fresh fruit or juice for the alcholic cocktail. One nutritionist says that on those evenings she comes home under tension, she cuts an orange and an apple in half. She bites hard first on an orange half and then on an apple half. By the time she completes the four halves of fruit, she is relaxed.

You can make some simple fruit concoctions to have on hand to greet you just inside the refrigerator door. Recipes follow:

Spiced Orange Slices

8 oranges
½ cup water
4 cups sugar
1 cup vinegar
10 whole cloves
2 (2-inch) sticks cinnamon

Cut oranges into half-inch slices; remove seeds and discard end pieces. Place oranges in heavy container and cover with ¼ cup water. Bring to a boil; reduce the heat, cover and simmer. Drain. Combine sugar, vinegar, ¼ cup water, cloves, and cinnamon in a container. Bring to a boil. Cook 5 minutes over medium heat, stirring constantly. Add drained orange slices. Remove from heat. Slices may garnish an entrée or may be packed in sterilized jars for future use. If storage is desired, after removing from heat, pack orange slices into hot, sterilized jars. Fill with syrup, to within one-half inch of jar top. Seal with parafin about one-eighth inch thick. Makes 4 pints or 30 to 40 slices.

Pineapple Delight

46 ounces canned pineapple juice, unsweetened

2 tablespoons lemon juice

6 ounces frozen concentrated orange juice

10 ounces club soda, chilled

mint leaves

Mix all ingredients. Makes 8 one-cup servings with 140 calories each.

Vegetable-Orange Cocktail

48 ounces vegetable juice cocktail

6 ounces frozen concentrated orange juice

¾ cup water

1 teaspoon basil leaves, crushed

Mix all ingredients. Chill. Makes 7 one-cup servings with 55 calories each.

Orange Nog

2 oranges peeled; cut in bite size slices

¼ cup nonfat skim milk

1 egg white

1 teaspoon sugar

2 ice cubes

Place all ingredients in an electric blender, blend until smooth. Makes 2 one-cup servings with 100 calories each.

Lemonade Syrup Base

1½ cups freshly squeezed lemon juice

2 teaspoons freshly grated lemon peel

1 cup boiling water

1 cup sugar

This is the lemonade syrup base. Dissolve sugar in boiling water. Add remaining ingredients. Store in covered container in refrigerator.

In a large glass, combine ¼ cup lemonade syrup base, ⅔ cup cold water, and ice cubes. Stir well. Makes 10 one-cup servings with 44 calories each.

New Orleans Punch

1½ cups milk

1½ cups light cream

½ cup white creme de cocoa

1 teaspoon vanilla

2 tablespoons powdered sugar

2 egg whites

cracked ice

ground cinnamon or nutmeg

Combine milk, light cream, creme de cocoa, vanilla, powdered sugar, and egg whites in blender container. Blend until frothy. Serve over cracked ice and sprinkle with cinnamon or nutmeg. Makes 4 one-cup servings with 110 calories each.

Coffee Punch

2 quarts hot strong coffee
½ cup sugar
2 cups milk
1½ teaspoons vanilla extract
1 quart vanilla ice cream

Combine coffee and sugar, stirring until dissolved. Chill. Combine coffee mixture, milk, and vanilla; mix well. Add ice cream, stirring gently. Ladle into serving cups. Garnish with whipped cream and mint leaf. Makes about 12 one-cup servings with 120 calories each.

Mint Julep

3 ounces lime flavored gelatin
1 cup very hot water
4 cups cold water
1 cup canned concentrated lemonade
1 cup crushed pineapple
mint sprigs

Empty into a bowl the 3 ounces lime gelatin. Add hot water and stir until thoroughlt dissolved. Add cold water and lemonade and stir, then add crushed pineapple. Garnish with sprigs. Makes 6 servings with 50 calories each cup.

Slush

6 ounces concentrated frozen orange juice
1 banana
12 ounces gingerale
3 cups water
12 ice cubes

Combine water, orange juice, banana, and ice cubes in electric blender. Blend until smooth. Combine orange juice mixture and gingerale, stir gently. Makes 5 one-cup servings with 100 calories each.

Orange Surprise

6 ounces frozen concentrated orange juice
1 cup milk
1 cup water
¼ cup sugar
½ teaspoon vanilla
ice cubes

Place all ingredients in a blender. Cover and blend until smooth. Makes 6 one-cup servings with 100 calories each.

Blossom Punch

⅓ cup concentrated frozen lemonade

⅓ cup concentrated frozen orange juice

1 eight ounce bottle chilled ginger ale

1½ teaspoons vanilla extract

1 quart vanilla ice cream

Combine all ingredients except for fruit slices, adding ginger ale last. Stir. Garnish with fruit slices. Makes 4 one-cup servings of 100 calories each.

Banana Milk

3 cups milk, whole or skim

2 eggs

¼ cup dehydrated (not diluted) milk

3 tablespoons dry yeast

1 banana

2 tablespoons honey

½ cup plain yogurt

Blend all ingredients. Makes 6 one-cup servings with 140 calories each.

Strawberry Daiquiri

4 cups strawberries, fresh or frozen (thawed)

6 ounces concentrated, frozen pink lemonade, diluted

1 teaspoon rum flavoring

cracked ice

Combine half of strwaberries, lemonade, and rum flavoring in blender. Blend until smooth. Add ice gradually until mixture is of desirable consistency. Pour into serving glasses. Repeat with remaining ingredients. Makes 6 one-cup servings with 100 calories each.

Frosty Peach

1 cup peach ice cream

1 teaspoon rum flavoring

3 tablespoons powdered sugar

3 fresh peaches, sliced unpealed

cracked ice

Combine ice cream, rum flavoring, sugar, and peaches in blender. Blend until smooth. Add ice and blend well. Makes 5 one-cup servings with 115 calories each.

Tropical Smoothee

1 cup fresh strawberries
1 quart frozen orange juice
2 bananas
6 ice cubes
whole strawberries

Combine ½ cup fresh strawberries, 1 pint orange juice, and one banana with 3 ice cubes in blender container. Blend until frothy and pour into stemmed glasses. Repeat with other half of ingredients, pouring into stemmed glasses. Garnish with whole strawberries. Makes 8 one-cup servings with 120 calories each.

Nutritious Snacks to Tide You Over

Every stress reliever hour needs some appetizer — good snacks; a fun time when friends meet and eat nutritious but low calorie foods. Just the sharing can be stress relieving. The recipes that follow are especially important because they are simple and easy to make.

Fruited Cheese Balls

8 ounces cream cheese, softened
1 cup crushed pineapple (fresh or canned)
2 cups chopped pecans
¼ cup green pepper
3 tablespoons chopped onions
⅛ teaspoon salt
1 teaspoon chopped chutney
fresh parsley
red or green grapes

Beat cream cheese slightly; gradually stir in pineapple, 1 cup pecans, green pepper, onion, salt, and chutney. Chill. Shape into a ball and roll in remaining pecans. Chill until ready to serve. Garnish with parsley and red or green grapes. Makes 4½ cups or one large ball — 35 calories each ½ inch slice.

Dips may be made with frozen vegetables or fresh vegetables; also fruits. They make very good stress reliever appetizers. You may want to try some of these with your favorite crackers or chips. Eat them slowly and count the number of dips. They all add up in calories.

Cucumber Dip

2 medium cucumbers, peeled, grated

8 ounces cream cheese, softened

½ teaspoon garlic salt

½ cup green pepper, finely chopped

1 tablespoon prepared Italian dressing or hot sauce

Drain cucumber and squeeze juice. Reserve juice. Beat cream cheese with small amount of cucumber juice until it is smooth. Add garlic salt, green pepper, and dressing. Stir in cucumber; chill. Makes 16 one-ounce servings of 25 calories each.

Spinach Spread

1¼ cups chopped spinach (fresh or frozen)

8 ounces cream cheese

3 tablespoons milk

2 tablespoons vegetable fat

⅛ teaspoon nutmeg

6 slices cooked bacon, crisp and crumbled

1¼ tablespoon lemon juice

⅛ teaspoon salt

Cook spinach until tender in very little water. Combine cream cheese, milk, and vegetable fat in top of double boiler; cook over low heat stirring constantly until cheese has melted amd mixture is smooth. Stir in nutmeg, bacon, lemon juice, and salt. Add spinach and stir. Chill. Makes 20 one-ounce servings with 25 calories each.

Salmon Fingers

7¾ ounces red salmon, drained and flaked

1 tablespoon finely chopped onion

3 tablespoons plain yogurt

4 slices whole wheat bread, toasted

¼ teaspoon dill weed

2 tablespoons vegetable fat

4 slices American cheese

In a bowl combine salmon, yogurt, onion, and dill weed. Mix well. Toast one side each slice of bread. Spread with vegetable fat. Spread each slice with equal portions of salmon mixture. Broil until hot. Top each with the cheese cut in small blocks. Broil until cheese begins to melt. Cut in finger-length pieces and serve immediately. Makes 16 finger strips of 25 calories each.

Cranberry Sausage Balls

1 pound seasoned bulk pack sausage

2 eggs, beaten

1 cup fresh bread crumbs

1 teaspoon salt

½ teaspoon poultry seasoning

16 ounces cranberry sauce

1 tablespoon prepared mustard

Combine sausage, eggs, bread crumbs, salt, and poultry seasoning. Shape into small 1-inch balls. Bake at 350 degrees for about 30 minutes. Combine cranberry sauce and mustard in saucepan; heat until melted. Add sausage balls. Cover and simmer about 15 minutes. Makes 35 meatballs of 30 calories each serving.

Tomato-Cheese Spread

1 cup fresh tomatoes, chopped
2 cups shredded cheddar cheese
8 ounces cream cheese, softened
½ cup vegetable fat, softened
⅓ cup onion, finely chopped
1 teaspoon salt
1½ cups pecans, chopped
parsley
cherry tomatoes

Combine tomatoes, cheddar cheese, cream cheese, vegetable fat, onion, and salt. Mix well. Shape into a log or ball (mixture will be soft). Roll in pecans. Place the log or ball on serving platter and bring ends together to make a ring. Cover. Chill for about 2 hours. Garnish with cherry tomatoes and parsley. Makes 30 one-ounce servings of 40 calories each.

Tomato and Onion Dip

1 medium tomato, finely chopped
½ cup lemon juice
½ teaspoon salt
¼ cup chopped onion
2 cups sour cream
¼ teaspoon Worcestershire sauce
½ teaspoon sugar

Mix tomato, lemon juice, salt; add onion, sour cream, sugar, and Worcestershire sauce and stir. Makes 24 one-ounce servings with 20 calories each.

Cherry tomatoes may be stuffed, using this recipe just change the lemon juice from ½ cup to 1 tablespoon.

Fresh Eggplant Sticks

1 large eggplant
all–purpose flour
salt
2 cups vegetable fat

Peel eggplant and cut into sticks about 2″ × ½″. Place sticks in salted water and allow to stand for about 1 hour. Drain eggplant sticks. Roll each stick in flour and fry in hot vegetable fat until golden brown; drain well. Serve while warm. Makes 25 to 30 sticks of 15 to 20 calories each.

Mushroom Cheddar Caps

1 pound fresh mushrooms

⅛ teaspoon salt

1 pound cheddar cheese, cubed

paprika

Rinse mushrooms and remove stems. Sprinkle cavities with salt. Place cheese cubes in each mushroom cavity. Sprinkle with paprika. Place mushrooms on baking sheet; broil until cheese bubbles, about 3 minutes. Makes 35 caps of 35 calories each cap.

Indian Canapés

1 cup smooth style peanut butter

9 ounces chutney, finely chopped

10 slices cooked bacon, crisp and crumbled

melba toast rounds

Combine peanut butter, chutney, and bacon. Stir until mixed. Place about 1 teaspoon of mixture on each toast round. Broil until hot. Makes 50 canapés with 25 calories each.

Artichoke Spread

2 cups artichoke hearts, chopped

1 cup mayonnaise

1 cup grated cheese, parmesan

curry powder

Steam artichoke hearts until tender. Drain. Combine artichoke hearts, mayonnaise, and cheese. Pour into baking dish. Sprinkle top with curry powder. Bake at 350 degrees for about 35 minutes. Serve warm. Makes 32 one-ounce servings with 30 calories each.

Bacon-and-Cheese Specials

3 slices cooked crisp bacon, finely chopped

1 teaspoon prepared mustard

¼ teaspoon paprika

4 ounces shredded sharp cheddar cheese

16 thin whole wheat slices

Combine bacon, mustard, paprika, and cheese. Toast bread on one side. Spread untoasted side of bread with 1 tablespoon of cheese mixture; cut into quarters. Broil squares until cheese melts. Serve immediately. Makes 64 squares with 30 calories each.

Cheese Tarts

8 ounces shredded sharp cheddar cheese

1 tablespoon nonfat (skim) milk

½ teaspoon dry mustard

¼ teaspoon paprika

½ teaspoon Worcestershire sauce

commercial tart shells

Combine cheese, milk, mustard, paprika, and Worcestershire sauce in top of double boiler; heat over the hot water until cheese melts, while stirring. Spoon into tart shells and allow to stand about 15 minutes before serving. Makes 24 tarts with 50 calories each.

Avocado Canapé

1 avocado, ripe (about 1 cup)

¼ cup onion or chives, chopped finely

⅛ teaspoon salt

1 tablespoon lemon juice

⅛ teaspoon chili powder

⅛ teaspoon celery salt

½ cup mayonnaise

Scoop out the pulp of a ripe avocado, mash, and season with onion or chives. Add salt, lemon juice, chili powder, and celery salt. Add mayonnaise and stir to a smooth paste. Makes 20 to 25 one-ounce servings of 25 calories each.

Broccoli Dip

10½ ounces fresh or frozen chopped broccoli

¼ cup vegetable fat

2 onions, chopped

2 cups chopped celery

½ cup canned mushroom stems and pieces, drained

3 ounces cream cheese

2½ cups cream of mushroom soup (homemade)

Cook broccoli slightly and drain. Melt vegetable fat; add onion, 1 cup celery, and broccoli and cook until onion is tender. Add mushrooms. Add 1 cup celery and cream cheese and cook over low heat until smooth and thick. Add mushroom soup. Serve hot in chafing dish. Makes 32 one-ounce servings of 25 calories each.

Minted Pineapple

2½ cups chunks of pineapple (fresh or canned), drained

white creme de menthe

shell of fresh watermelon

fresh mint sprigs or leaves

cluster of red grapes

Cover pineapple chunks with creme de menthe. May be served in watermelon shell. Chill before serving. Garnish with fresh mint leaves and red grape clusters. Wooden picks will make the fruit easy to serve. Makes about 15 one-ounce servings of 25 calories each.

Instead of a dip, vegetables or fruits make excellent spreads. Serve these with your favorite crackers.

Starting Out with a Good Breakfast

All the nutritionists felt that much stress is prevented by beginning your day with exercise and a good breakfast. Feeling good, thinking positive thoughts, and looking your best early in the day goes far toward keeping you in good health.

The following good breakfasts are quick to fix, simple, but a nourishing 300 calories each.

½ cup orange juice

1 tablespoon peanut butter

1 slice whole wheat toast

tea or coffee

½ cup grapefruit juice
   or
   grapefruit half

blueberry muffin with vegetable fat

½ glass nonfat milk

hot tea with lemon

½ cup vegetable juice with lemon

½ cup cereal with ½ banana

½ cup nonfat milk

tea or coffee

½ cup fruit sections

3 ounces cottage cheese with pineapple chunks

1 slice raisin toast

coffee

Eating Foods in Their Natural Form

Teaching nutritionists suggest eating foods in their natural form, fresh and raw, to get the most nutrition. For vegetables that need to be cooked, steam them until crisp tender. If you must simmer them, use the smallest amount of water possible.

Canned or dried fruit is usually more economical, and can be stored. When using the canned fruit, save the juice and use it as the liquid in gelatin. This will make the gelatin more nutritious. Pineapple juice because of its medium pectin count will make a softer gelatin. For a stiffer product combine it with pear or peach juice.

Vegetable juices are flavorful, nutritious additions to soups.

Using Common Sense and Moderation

Nutritionists agree that we should all use good and constant nutrition sense, especially when under stress. If you favor fats over carbohydrates (sugars and starches), you may want to consider the results of eating each.

Fat yields more energy per ounce than carbohydrates and gives you a feeling of fullness since it remains in your stomach longer. Fat is fat, however, and can become stored as body fat.

Carbohydrates in complex form, on the other hand, are much more healthy energy sources, the nutritionists agree. The complex form will not only satisfy energy needs but contain other food nutrients needed by the body such as protein, minerals, and vitamins.

Research at the University of Virginia has proven that complex carbohydrates are a better source of energy than protein. In studies where two groups of rats were given equal calorie diets — one high in protein, the other high in carbohydrates — the animals that consumed the high carbohydrate diet stored less body fat and gained less weight than the animals on the high protein diet.

Nutritionists believe that in a balanced diet at least 55 to 60 percent of the calories should be from complex carbohydrate sources. They recommend you include whole-grain bread in each meal — the amount determined by the total calories needs of your body.

Nutritionists Recommend:

We have discussed some nutritionists' thoughts on relieving stress. Nutritionists, through organizations such as the American Dietetic Association and Society for Nutrition Education, have expressed support for the Dietary Guidelines set forth in the 1980 publications of the U.S. Department of Agriculture and the U.S. Department of Health and Human Services. We are promoting the importance of nutrition in promoting and maintaining good health.

Our recommendations:

- Eat a variety of foods
- Maintain your ideal weight
- Avoid too many saturated fats
- Eat complex carbohydrates (choose ones with most food nutrients and fibers)
- Avoid sugar
- Avoid sodium and salt
- Practice moderation in food and alcohol
- Eat a proper diet (one planned for your individual needs).

Daily, you should:

- Be aware of your body's need for food and the foods you eat
- Follow proper diet
- Eat high-quality foods — those providing most nutrition.
- Eat as many fresh foods as possible.
- Select foods wisely when you eat out
- Eat a variety of foods in moderation
- Eat frequent small meals if under stress or doing sedentary work
- Begin each day with a good breakfast
- Chew all foods thoroughly
- Drink plenty of water

Some other good health practices:

- Exercise each day
- Get plenty of sleep
- Pace yourself by your body's abilities
- Allow for a relaxation time each day
- Know yourself and your stress threshold to prevent stress and stress effects
- Practice moderation in all things.

A Simple Relaxing Dinner for Six

Still thinking, "I am too busy to eat the way I should," or, "I'm no gourmet and my family's lucky I get anything on the table at all."? Then take heed of the nutritionists queried who all say any average person with a normal amount of time for food preparation can prepare a nutritionally well-balanced meal.

Take the plunge and try this sample dinner for six.

Sunday Dinner for Six

Chilled vegetable juice with celery stirrers

Assorted cheese

Baked sweet and sour chicken

Elegant broccoli

Stuffed baked tomato halves

California green salad

Blueberry muffins

Orange — date mallow

Ice tea or coffee

Elegant Broccoli

20 ounces frozen broccoli spears
½ cup melted vegetable fat
2 tablespoons lemon juice
½ cup chopped toasted almonds

Cook broccoli until barely tender. Drain. Combine vegetable fat and lemon juice. Arrange broccoli in a bowl. Top with vegetable fat and lemon juice mixture. Sprinkle with almonds. Makes 6 servings of 100 calories each.

Stuffed Baked Tomato Half

3 large tomatoes
1½ teaspoons salt
1 teaspoon prepared mustard
1 teaspoon chopped onion
1 tablespoon chopped parsley
1 tablespoon chopped celery leaves
1 teaspoon whole oregano
1 teaspoon vegetable fat

Wash tomatoes, remove stem end and cut crosswise in half. Sprinkle tomatoes with salt and spread with mustard. Combine onion, parsley, celery leaves, and oregano. Sprinkle over tomatoes. Dot each half with vegetable fat. Bake at 350 degrees for about 30 minutes or until tender. Makes 6 servings of 75 calories each.

Sweet-Sour Baked Chicken

3 2½ pound chicken broiler fryers, cut in quarters
salt
½ cup vegetable oil
½ cup honey
½ teaspoon paprika
1 teaspoon dry mustard

Rub each piece of chicken with salt. Arrange skin side down in greased baking pan. Combine oil, honey, lemon juice, paprika, and mustard in small bowl. Baste chicken with sauce. Cover and bake at 375 degrees for 30 minutes. Turn chicken and brush with sauce. Bake uncovered at 400 degrees for about 20 minutes until tender. Makes 6 servings of 150 calories each.

Orange-Date Mallow

1½ cups mandarin orange sections
½ cup pitted dates, quartered
1 cup miniature marshmallows
½ cup pecan halves
⅔ cup whipped topping
¼ cup toasted graham cracker crumbs

Drain orange sections, reserving 2 tablespoons juice for later use. Combine orange sections, dates, marshmallows, and pecans. Toss lightly. Blend whipped topping and reserved orange juice. Mix with fruit mixture. Chill. Garnish each serving with toasted coconut or serve over graham cracker crumb base. Makes 6 servings of 75 calories each.

Blueberry Muffins

1¾ cups all-purpose flour
1 tablespoon baking powder
½ teaspoon salt
¼ cup sugar
1 egg
1 cup milk
3 tablespoons melted vegetable fat
1 cup fresh blueberries, or ¾ cup drained canned blueberries
2 tablespoons all-purpose flour

Mix 1¾ cups flour, baking powder, salt, and sugar. Make a well in center of dry ingredients. Beat egg until light, add milk and vegetable fat. Pour liquid into well and stir until dry ingredients are moistened. Combine the blueberries and 2 tablespoons flour; add to muffin mixture. Fill muffin pans one-half full. Bake at 425 degrees for 25 minutes. Makes 12 muffins of 85 calories each.

California Green Salad

1 large head iceberg lettuce
¼ teaspoon garlic salt
2 avocados, peeled and diced
Italian dressing

Tear lettuce into bite-size pieces in salad bowl. Add garlic salt. Toss lightly with dressing to coat the leaves. Add avocado. Toss lightly and serve. Makes 6 servings of 50 calories each.

Favorite Recipes from Nutritionists

Finally, here are some additional recipes recommended by nutritionists. The next time you are tempted to reach for a high carbohydrate substitute for a full meal or to take the family out for a high calorie fast food meal, take a look at these tempting selections: Main courses such as Stuffed Chicken Breasts or Lemon Broiled Fillets; vegetable sidedishes like Green Beans and Mushrooms or Sweet and Sour Cucumbers; breads including Parmesan Sticks and Spoonbread; crisp salads and quick desserts will change your mind.

Entrees

Florentine Rice

2 cups spinach, chopped and blended in an electric blender
1 cup sharp cheddar cheese, shredded
1 cup cooked rice
2 eggs, slightly beaten
2 tablespoons soft vegetable fat
½ cup milk
2 tablespoons onion, chopped
½ teaspoon Worcestershire sauce
½ teaspoon salt
¼ teaspoon rosemary, crushed

Combine spinach, cheese, rice, eggs, vegetable fat, milk, onion, Worcestershire sauce, salt, and rosemary and mix together thoroughly. Pour into baking dish about 3 inches deep. Bake at 350 degrees about 35 minutes. Cut in wedge shape and serve. Makes 6 servings of 175 calories each.

Beef Fondue

1 pound sirloin tip, boneless, cut in strips or cubes
    about ¾" thick

1⅓ cups browned mushroom sauce (see recipe
    to follow)

1 cup vegetable fat

6 cups vegetable oil

Trim off all fat from meat. Place meat in pan and chill. Prepare the mushroom sauce for dipping. About 25-30 minutes before serving, heat vegetable fat and vegetable oil in a saucepan. When mixture begins to bubble pour into a fondue pot. Place fondue pot on stand and light canned heat or use an electric pot. When fat begins to bubble, place a piece of beef on a fork and dip in hot oil. Allow to cook 2 to 3 minutes. Place meat on individual plates. Dip meat cube in brown mushroom sauce. 4 strips makes 1 serving of 150 calories each.

Browned Mushroom Sauce

2 tablespoons vegetable fat

2 tablespoons all-purpose flour

⅔ cup consommé

1 teaspoon Worcestershire sauce

½ cup sour cream

½ cup mushrooms, finely chopped

Melt vegetable fat in a saucepan. Stir in flour. Remove from heat. Gradually stir in consommé. Return to heat and cook until thickened. Stir in Worcestershire sauce, mushrooms, and sour cream. Serve hot. Serves 5 to 6 (sauce and meat) of 125 calories each.

Lemon-Broiled Fillets

2 pounds fish fillets, fresh or frozen

2 tablespoons vegetable oil

2 tablespoons soy sauce

2 tablespoons Worcestershire sauce

½ teaspoon chili powder

1 teaspoon paprika

½ teaspoon garlic powder

lemon wedges

If frozen fish is used, allow to thaw. Place fillets in a single layer, skin side down. Grease broiler pan with the vegetable fat. Mix soy sauce, Worcestershire sauce, chili powder, paprika, and garlic powder. Pour the mixture over the fillets. Broil for about 15 minutes or until fillets are tender. Baste once during process with sauce in pan. Serve on platter. Garnish with lemon wedges. Makes 6 servings of 125 calories each.

Oriental Beef With Peppers

1 pound sirloin tip, boneless, cut in thin strips 2" × 1"

½ cup vegetable fat

1 cup green peppers, cut in 2" pieces

1 cup onion quarters

1 teaspoon salt

Brown sirloin strips in pan in vegetable fat. When strips are done add green peppers and onions and cook until barely tender. Add salt and stir. Cover and allow to simmer for about 10 minutes. Serve hot over rice. Makes 5 servings of 130 calories each.

Chicken and Mushroom Casserole

1 cup mushrooms, fresh or canned
1 3-pound chicken cut into serving pieces
1 cup unsweetened pineapple chunks
1 small green pepper, seeded and cut into strips
¼ cup diced onion
1 tablespoon cornstarch
1¼ teaspoon salt
½ teaspoon ground ginger
3 medium carrots, peeled
½ cup chicken broth

If mushrooms are fresh, rinse, dry, and slice; if canned, drain and set aside. Arrange chicken on broiler pan and place in broiler oven for about 8 minutes on each side; turn over. Pour off pan drippings. Place chicken pieces in a 3-quart casserole dish. Drain and reserve liquid from pineapple, set aside. Place mushrooms, pineapple, green pepper, and onion over chicken. Mix pineapple liquid with cornstarch, salt, and ginger. Pour over casserole. Bake in preheated oven at 350 degrees for about 60 minutes until chicken is tender. Peel and slice carrots in thin slices. Place chicken broth in saucepan. Add carrots and cook until crisp tender. Drain. Serve chicken casserole on platter. Garnish with carrot slices. Makes 4 servings of 40 calories each.

Beef and Applesauce Loaf

1 beaten egg
1 cup breadcrumbs
1¼ cups applesauce
2 tablespoons chopped onions
2 teaspoons prepared mustard
1 teaspoon dried celery flakes
½ teaspoon salt
1 tablespoon brown sugar
1 tablespoon vinegar
¼ teaspoon ground allspice

Mix egg, bread crumbs, ½ cup applesauce, onion, 1 teaspoon mustard, celery flakes, and salt. Add ground beef. Mix well. Shape into a round loaf in a shallow baking dish, leaving a depression in the top of the loaf. Combine the remaining ½ cup applesauce, 1 teaspoon mustard. Stir in brown sugar, vinegar and allspice. Fill depression with the mixture. Bake at 350 degrees for about 60 minutes. Makes 8 servings of 150 calories each.

Stuffed Chicken Breasts

1 cup fresh spinach leaves chopped
1 cup ricotta cheese
½ cup diced mozzarella cheese
½ teaspoon salt
¼ teaspoon dried thyme
½ teaspoon dried tarragon
4 whole, boned chicken breasts, leave on skin
4 tablespoons vegetable fat, softened

Mix spinach, ricotta, and mozzarella cheese with salt, thyme, and tarragon in a large bowl. Divide mixture evenly among breasts. Lift up skin of each chicken breast and stuff. Smooth skin over stuffing and gently tuck skin and flesh underneath, forming a neat plump piece. Rub each stuffed breast with vegetable fat. Place chicken breasts in a greased roasting pan and bake in preheated oven at 350 degrees for about 1 hour. Baste breasts with juices in pan at least twice. When done, breasts may be served hot, garnished with your favorite vegetable, or chilled and then sliced thinly or in halves. Makes 8 servings with 90 calories in each serving.

Beef-Celery Bake

1 bunch celery
½ cup water
2½ teaspoons salt
1½ cups cottage cheese
4 eggs
2½ teaspoons Italian seasoning
2 teaspoons onion powder
1 pound ground beef
2 cups tomatoes, whole drained and broken up
2 ounces mozzarella cheese, sliced thinly

Preheat oven to 325 degrees. Cut celery to one-quarter-inch slices. In a medium saucepan, place the water and 1 teaspoon salt and heat to a boil. Add celery. Cook covered until almost tender, about 8 minutes. Drain. In a bowl, mix cottage cheese, 3 eggs, Italian seasonings, ½ teaspoon salt, and 1 teaspoon onion powder. Brown the beef in a skillet. Stir. Drain off drippings. Stir in remaining 1 teaspoon salt, one teaspoon onion powder, Italian seasoning, tomatoes, and the 1 egg. Place half of the celery in a casserole dish. Spread half of the cottage cheese on top. Cover with half of the ground beef and repeat with layers until all products have been placed in casserole dish. Cover with the mozzarella cheese. Makes 6 one-half cup servings with 150 calories each.

Chicken Citrus

3 boned chicken breasts, halved, skinned and flattened

½ cup melted vegetable fat

1 tablespoon orange juice

6 thin slices cooked ham

½ cup flour

2 slightly beaten eggs

⅔ cup fine bread crumbs

½ cup vegetable fat, cut in bits

2 cups fresh orange juice

1 tablespoon tarragon

1 teaspoon grated orange peel

½ teaspoon salt

6 ½-inch thick orange slices

Place chicken breast halves on a flat surface, smooth side down, in preheated oven at 400 degrees. Brush with melted vegetable fat mixed with 1 tablespoon orange juice. Place one slice of ham on each breast and roll up; secure with toothpicks. Roll in flour. Dip in beaten egg and then roll in bread crumbs. Place in a greased baking dish. Dot with bits of vegetable fat. Bake for 15 minutes, turning once. Combine orange juice, tarragon, orange peel, and salt. Pour over chicken. Reduce temperature to 350 degrees. Cover and bake 35 minutes longer. Baste occasionally. Remove toothpicks from chicken. Place each chicken piece on an orange slice on a serving platter. Pour sauce over chicken. Garnish with orange peel grated and minced parsley. Makes 6 servings of 195 calories each.

Vegetables

Mandarin Beets

1 ½ cups mandarin orange sections, undrained

orange juice (fresh) to make up juice from manderin sections

¼ cup vegetable fat

¼ teaspoon ground ginger

¼ teaspoon ground nutmeg

1 ½ tablespoons cornstarch

2 tablespoons water

½ teaspoon salt

2 cups sliced beets, fresh or canned, cooked, drained

Drain orange sections. Add enough orange juice to make 1 ½ cups. Heat orange juice, vegetable fat, ginger, and nutmeg in saucepan. Dissolve cornstarch in water. Add cornstarch to juice mixture at boiling point. Add salt. Stir constantly until sauce thickens. Add orange sections. Add sliced beets. Heat and serve. Garnish with orange sections. Makes 6 one-half cup servings of 65 calories each.

Green Beans and Mushrooms

⅓ cup Italian dressing

½ teaspoon grated fresh lemon peel

1 tablespoon fresh squeezed lemon juice

1 ¼ cups cut green beans, frozen or fresh, cooked, drained

¼ cup sliced fresh or canned mushrooms, cooked, drained

Combine Italian dressing, lemon peel, and lemon juice. Add green beans and mushrooms. Heat. Makes 3 to 4 servings of 60 calories each.

Lemon Parmesan Cauliflower

1 medium head cauliflower, broken into flowerets
juice of 1 fresh lemon
2 tablespoons grated Parmesan cheese
¼ teaspoon paprika
¼ teaspoon salt
2 tablespoons vegetable fat, melted

Place cauliflower head in about ¼ cup water and cook until tender (about 20 minutes). If flowerets, cook about 10 minutes. Add juice of ½ lemon before cooking. Mix Parmesan cheese and paprika. Sprinkle over cauliflower. Add salt. Before serving, sprinkle on remaining juice of ½ lemon and vegetable fat. Garnish with lemon cartwheel twists and parsley. Makes 4 servings of 55 calories each.

Asparagus with Cheese Sauce

2 cups or 16 ounces asparagus spears (fresh or frozen) cooked
½ cup milk
2 cups processed cheese, diced
1 teaspoon salt
1 teaspoon Worcestershire sauce
2 teaspoons prepared mustard
paparika

Heat asparagus and the liquid it was cooked in. Mix milk and cheese. Heat slowly. Stir until blended. Add salt, Worcestershire sauce, and mustard. Drain asparagus and place in serving dish. Top with cheese sauce. Garnish with paparika. Makes 6 servings of 70 calories each.

Sweet-and-Sour Cucumbers

6 cucumbers, medium size, peeled
1 cup white vinegar
¾ cup sugar
1 teaspoon salt
2 teaspoons red-wine vinegar

Cut cucumbers lengthwise. Scrape out seeds, if desired. Slice cucumbers about one-eighth inch thick. Place in serving dish. Mix white vinegar, sugar, salt, and wine vinegar in a bowl. Pour mixture over cucumber slices. Allow to set about 10 minutes before serving. Makes 3-4 one-half cup servings of 45 calories each.

Glazed Carrots

4 cups cooked carrots, sliced
¼ cup vegetable fat
1½ tablespoons sugar
3 tablespoons fresh or frozen and reconstituted orange juice
6 whole cloves
¼ teaspoon salt

Heat carrots to steaming. Combine vegetable fat, sugar, orange juice, cloves, and salt in saucepan. Heat until sugar is dissolved and vegetable fat melted. Serve carrots in serving dish. Pour sauce over carrots. Garnish with chopped parsley. Makes 6 one-half cup servings of 60 calories each.

Herbed Vegetables

2½ cups whole baby carrots, frozen or canned

1⅛ cups (10 ounces) broccoli spears, frozen or fresh, cooked tender

1⅛ cups green beans

1 red onion, thinly sliced into rings

½ cup vegetable oil

½ cup vinegar

2 tablespoons lemon juice

½ teaspoon rosemary, crushed

1 clove garlic, crushed

¼ cup chopped parsley

½ teaspoon Italian seasoning

Cook vegtables separately until crisp and tender. Drain. Arrange attractively on a platter. Top with onion rings. Mix oil with vinegar, lemon juice, rosemary, clove garlic, parsley, and Italian seasoning. Pour over vegetables. Refrigerate several hours before serving. Makes 8 servings of 85 calories each.

Mixed Vegetable Sautée

4 green peppers, cut in strips

3 onions, medium size, sliced

4 stalks celery, sliced

4 tablespoons vegetable fat

1 cup sliced mushrooms, cooked and drained

¼ teaspoon salt

Sauté peppers, onions, and celery in melted vegetable fat until barely tender. Cover and simmer about 5 minutes. Add mushrooms. Stir. Add salt and stir. Makes 6 servings of 65 calories each.

Breads

Spoonbread

1 cup cornmeal

3 cups milk

1 teaspoon salt

1 teaspoon baking powder

2 tablespoons vegetable oil

3 eggs, separated

Combine cornmeal with 2 cups milk in saucepan. Stir. Cook until consistency is mushy. Remove from heat. Add salt, baking powder, oil and 1 cup milk. Beat egg yolks well. Stir into warm mixture. Beat egg whites until stiff peaks form. Fold into cornmeal mixture.

Pour into greased casserole dish. Bake at 325 degrees for 1 hour. Serve hot. Makes 6 servings of 100 calories each.

Hot-Buttered French Bread

½ cup vegetable fat

2 teaspoons parsley flakes

1 sixteen-ounce loaf French or Italian bread

Melt vegetable fat. Add parsley flakes. Cut bread into thin slices, leaving loaf intact at bottom. Brush mixture between slices and on top of bread. Wrap in foil. Bakes at 350 degrees until hot. Makes 8 servings of 90 calories each.

Cheese Biscuits

2 cups all-purpose flour
½ teaspoon salt
2 teaspoons baking powder
¾ cup grated cheddar cheese
¼ cup vegetable fat
¾ cup milk

Combine flour, salt and baking powder. Cut in cheese and vegetable fat. Add milk and stir carefully until dry ingredients are moist. Stir until mixture forms a soft dough. Drop from teaspoon onto greesed baking sheet. Bake at 425 degrees for about 15 minutes. Makes 12 biscuits with 50 calories each.

Parmesan Sticks

6 slices bread, whole grain
¼ cup grated, Parmesan cheese
½ cup cornflake crumbs
¼ teaspoon garlic salt
¼ cup vegetable fat, melted

Trim crust from bread. Cut each slice of bread into 4 strips. Combine cheese, crumbs, and garlic salt. Dip bread strips in vegetable fat. Roll in crumb mixture. Place on baking sheet. Bake at 425 degrees for 7 minutes. Makes 6 servings of 70 calories each.

Peanut–Butter Bread

4½ cups all-purpose flour
2 tablespoons baking powder
1¼ teaspoon salt
⅔ cup sugar
1 cup peanut butter
2 eggs, beaten
2 cups milk
1 tablespoon grated orange rind
½ cup chopped unsalted peanuts

Mix flour, baking powder, salt, and sugar in a bowl. Add peanut butter, cutting it into mixture until mixture is coarse. Combine eggs, milk, orange rind, and chopped peanuts. Stir into mixture. Pour batter into greased loaf pan about 9″ × 5″ × 3″. Bake for 1 hour at 350 degrees. When done turn out on wire rack to cool. Wrap in foil and store overnight before slicing. Makes 9 servings of 70 calories each.

Note: other foods can be substituted for peanut butter such as banana, sweet potato, raisins and dates.

Salads

Vegetable Dressing

1½ teaspoons paprika
½ teaspoon celery salt
1 teaspoon salt
2 tablespoons sugar
½ cup vegetable oil
¼ cup wine vinegar
1 tablespoon chopped parsley
1 small onion, chopped

Combine paprika, celery salt, and sugar in mixing bowl. Add one half of vegetable oil. Beat until thoroughly mixed. Add 1 tablespoon vinegar. Beat. Repeat process, alternating oil and vinegar. Add parsley and onion. Mix. Allow to stand or store in refrigerator in covered container. Serve over vegetables. Makes 8 one ounce servings with 45 calories each.

Spinach Salad

½ cup pineapple chunks, fresh or canned, in unsweetened pineapple juice, drained
¼ cup sliced celery
¼ cup sliced radishes
2 tablespoons sliced green onion
1 cup cooked chicken, cubed
2 cups fresh spinach, torn to bite size pieces

In a large salad bowl, mix pineapple chunks, celery, radishes, and green onion. Add cubed chicken. Mix. Toss in fresh spinach. Serve on salad plates. Makes 2 one-half cup servings of 80 calories each.

Fruit Dressing

⅓ cup sugar
1 teaspoon salt
½ teaspoon paprika
¼ cup orange juice
3 tablespoons lemon juice
1 tablespoon vinegar
¾ cup vegetable oil

Combine all ingredients in a jar. Shake. Serve on fruits, avocado slices, apples, or green vegetables. Makes 10 one-ounce servings of 55 calories each.

Fruit Salad Ambrosia

2 cups fresh or canned pineapple chunks, drained
1½ cups canned mandarin oranges, drained
2 bananas, sliced
½ cup grapes
½ cup miniature marshmallows
¼ cup whipped cream
1 tablespoon mayonnaise
lettuce
3 tablespoons lemon juice
shredded coconut

Combine pineapple, orange sections, bananas, grapes, and marshmallows. Stir. Add whipped cream and mayonnaise. Serve on lettuce bed. Sprinkle lemon juice over top. Garnish with shredded coconut. Makes 6 one-half cup servings of 100 calories each.

Orange Pudding Puff

| 6 eggs, separated |
| 1¾ cup sugar |
| ¼ cup cornstarch |
| ¼ teaspoon salt |
| 1 quart milk |
| 1 teaspoon vanilla extract |
| 8 oranges, peeled, chopped, drained |

Beat egg yolks; set aside. Mix one cup of sugar, cornstarch, and salt in heavy saucepan. Stir. Add milk. Cook to boiling but do not boil. Stir constantly. Remove from heat. Gradually stir into beaten egg yolks. Stir constantly. Cook until smooth and thickened. Stir in vanilla. Pour into large mixing bowl and chill. Stir orange pieces into custard. Beat egg whites until foamy, gradually add ¾ cups sugar, 1 tablespoon at a time, beating until stiff peaks form. Fold egg whites into the custard. Serve immediately. Makes 12 one-half cup servings of 150 calories each.

Pineapple Sherbet

| 2½ cups buttermilk |
| 1 cup crushed canned pineapple, undrained |
| 2 tablespoons honey |
| ½ cup fresh orange juice |
| ½ cup fresh lemon juice |
| ½ cup light corn syrup |
| ⅔ cup sugar |

Combine buttermilk, crushed pineapple, honey, orange juice, lemon juice, corn syrup, and sugar. Place in freezer pan and allow to freeze, then stir. Place in electric freezer and freeze. Let stand about 1 hour. Makes 10 to 12 one-half cup servings of 175 calories each.

Raspberry Parfait

| 1 cup unflavored gelatin |
| 2 tablespoons sugar |
| 1¼ cup fresh or frozen raspberries, reserve liquid |
| ½ cup water |
| 2 cups red tropical fruit punch (frozen, reconstituted, or canned) |
| 1 cup plain yogurt |

Mix unflavored gelatin and sugar. Blend in raspberry liquid with water. Stir until gelatin dissolves. Pour into bowl. Add fruit punch. In small bowl, combine yogurt with ¾ cup gelatin mixture. Blend. To remaining gelatin mixture add 1 cup fruit punch. Chill both mixtures. Fold in raspberries into plain gelatin mixture.

Serve in parfait glasses alternate layer of raspberry, then yogurt mixture. Chill. Allow to set for several hours. Makes 8 one-half cup servings of 85 calories each.

Peach Ice

| 2 cups fresh peaches or frozen |
| 1½ cups pineapple juice concentrate, undiluted |
| ⅛ teaspoon almond extract |

Combine peaches, pineapple juice, and almond extract in blender. Blend until smooth. Stir occasionally. Pour into freezer container and freeze until firm. Serve in dishes. Makes 6 one-half cup servings of 110 calories each.

Lime Pie —
Low in Calories

1 cup lime gelatin (1 package)
½ teaspoon salt
2 teaspoons grated fresh lime rind
½ cup fresh lime juice
1½ cups milk, nonfat
3 eggs, separated
¼ cup fresh coconut
vanilla wafers, crushed to make crust

Mix gelatin, ¼ teaspoon salt, grated lime rind in double boiler. Add lime juice, milk, ¼ teaspoon salt and beaten egg yolks. Cook over boiling water until gelatin melts and mixture coats metal spoon. Remove from heat. Chill until mixture gets very thick but not set. Beat egg whites to peak. Add coconut. Pour mixture into 9 inch pie crust (vanilla wafers). Top with meringue. Sprinkle top with coconut. Allow to chill for several hours. Makes 6 servings of 200 calories each.

Appendix

Food Exchanges

Food exchanges allow for variety in meal planning. You will be able to maintain your diet, yet vary it from day to day.

Food exchanges are based on the comparable calorie content of foods. Within a food group, an item high in calories is reduced in quantity to equal an item lower in calories. Therefore, if you wish to have something other than 1 cup of orange juice with breakfast, you can refer to the Fruit Exchange List and choose instead one small apple or ½ a banana and know it equals 40 calories.

The purpose of the food exchange list is to allow flexibility in calorie or fat–controlled diets.

The food exchanges have been used successfully in treating diabetes by diet alone, and the weight-watching person can eat most foods, provided it is in the prescribed amounts.

Adapted from Food Exchange List for Meal Planning, The American Dietetic Association.

Meat Exchanges

One Exchange of lean meat (1 oz.) contains 7 grams of protein, 3 grams of fat and 55 calories.

Beef:	baby beef (very lean), chipped beef, chuck, flank steak, tenderloin, plate ribs, plate skirt steak, round (bottom, top), all cuts rump, sirloin, tripe.	1 oz.
Lamb:	leg, rib, sirloin, loin (roast and chops), shank, shoulder	1 oz.
Pork:	leg, (whole, rump, center shank), ham, smoked (center slices)	1 oz.
Veal:	leg, loin, rib, shank, shoulder, cutlets	1 oz.
Poultry:	meat without skin of chicken, turkey, cornish hen, guinea hen, phesant	1 oz.
Fish:	any fresh or frozen canned	1 oz.
	salmon, tuna, mackerel, crab and lobster,	¼ cup
	clams, oysters, scallops, shrimp,	5 or 1 oz.
	sardines, drained	3
Cheeses containing less than 5% butterfat		1 oz.
cottage cheese, dry and 2% butterfat		¼ cup
dried beans and peas (omit 1 bread exchange)		½ cup

Bread Exchanges

Bread, cereal and starchy vegetables

One exchange of bread contains 15 grams of carbohydrate, 2 grams of protein and 70 calories.

Bread

White (including French and Italian)	1 slice
Whole wheat	1 slice
Rye or pumpernickel	1 slice
Raisin	1 slice
Bagal, small	½
English muffin, small	½
Plain roll, bread	1
Frankfurter roll	½
Hamburger bun	½
Dried bread crumbs	3 Tbs.
Tortilla, 6″	1

Cereal

Bran flakes	½ cup
Other ready-to-eat unsweetened cereal	¾ cup
puffed cereal (unfrosted)	1 cup
Cereal (cooked)	½ cup
Grits (cooked)	½ cup
Rice or Barley (cooked)	½ cup
Pasta (cooked), spaghetti noodles, macaroni	½ cup
Popcorn (popped, no fat added)	3 cups
Cornmeal (dry)	2 Tbs.
Flour	2½ Tbs.
Wheat Germ	¼ cup

Crackers

Arrowroot	3
Graham, 2½" sq.	2
Matzoth, 4"x6"	½
Oyster	20
Pretzels, 3⅛" long x ⅛ dia.	25
Rye Wafers, 2"x3½"	3
Saltines	6
Soda, 2½" sq.	4

Dried Beans, Peas and Lentils

Beans, Peas, Lentils (dried and cooked)	½ cup
Baked Beans no pork (canned)	¼ cup

Starchy Vegetables

Corn	⅓ cup
Corn on Cob	1 small
Lima Beans	½ cup
Parsnips	⅔ cup
Peas, Green (canned or frozen)	½ cup
Potato, white	1 small
Potato (mashed)	½ cup
Pumpkin	¾ cup
Winter squash, Acorn or Butternut	½ cup
Yam or Sweet Potato	¼ cup

Prepared Foods

Biscuit 2" dia. (omit 1 fat exchange)	1
Corn Bread, 2" x 2" x 1" (omit 1 fat exchange)	1
Corn Muffin, 2" dia. (omit 1 fat exchange)	1
Crackers, round butter type (omit 1 fat exchange)	5
Muffin, plain small (omit 1 fat exchange)	1
Potatoes, French Fried, Length 2" to 3½" (omit 1 fat exchange)	8
Potato or Corn Chips (omit 2 fat exchanges)	15
Pancake, 5" x ½" (omit 1 fat exchange)	1
Waffle, 5" x ½" (omit 1 fat exchange)	1

Fat Exchanges

One exchange of fat contains 5 grams of fat and 45 calories.

Margarine, soft, tub or stick*	1 teaspoon
Avocado (4″ in diameter)**	⅛
Oil: corn, cottonseed, safflower, soy, sunflower	1 teaspoon
Oil, olive**	1 teaspoon
Oil, peanut**	1 teaspoon
Olives**	5 small
Almonds**	10 whole
Pecans**	2 large whole
Peanuts**	
Spanish	20 whole
Virginia	10 whole
Walnuts	6 small
Nuts, other**	6 small
Margarine, regular stick	1 teaspoon
Butter	1 teaspoon
Bacon fat	1 teaspoon
Bacon, crisp	1 strip
Cream, light	2 tablespoons
Cream, sour	2 tablespoons
Cream, heavy	1 tablespoon
Cream cheese	1 tablespoon
French dressing***	1 tablespoon
Italian dressing***	1 tablespoon
Lard	1 teaspoon
Mayonnaise***	1 teaspoon
Salad dressing, mayonnaise type***	2 teaspoons
Salt pork	¾ inch cube

*Make with corn, cottonseed, safflower, soy or sunflower oil only

**Fat content is primarily monnounsaturated

***If made with corn, cottonseed, safflower, soy or sunflower oil can be used on fat modified diet.

Milk Exchanges

One exchange of milk contains 12 grams of carbohydrate, 8 grams of protein, a trace of fat and 80 calories.

Nonfat Fortified Milk

Nonfat or skim milk	1 cup
Powdered (nonfat dry, before adding liquid)	⅓ cup
Canned, evaporated—nonfat or skim milk	½ cup
Buttermilk made from nonfat milk	1 cup
Yogurt made from nonfat milk (plain, unflavored)	1 cup

Lowfat fortified milk

1% fat fortified milk (omit ½ fat exchange)	1 cup
2% fat fortified milk (omit 1 fat exchange)	1 cup
Yogurt made from 2% fortified milk (plain, unflavored) (omit 1 fat exchange)	1 cup

Whole milk (omit 2 fat exchanges)

Whole milk	1 cup
Canned, evaporated whole milk	½ cup
Buttermilk made from whole milk	1 cup
Yogurt made from whole milk (plain, unflavored)	1 cup

Vegetable Exchanges

(all non-starchy vegetables)

One exchange of vegetables contains about 5 grams of carbohydrate, 2 grams of protein and 25 calories. One exchange is ½ cup.

Asparagus
Bean Sprouts
Beets
Broccoli
Brussels Sprouts
Cabbage
Carrots
Cauliflower
Celery
Eggplant
Green pepper
Greens:
  Beet
  Chards
  Collards
  Dandelion
  Kale
  Mustard
  Spinach
  Turnip

Mushrooms
Okra
Onions
Rhubarb
Rutabaga
Sauerkraut
String beans, green or yellow
Summer squash
Tomatoes
Tomato juice
Turnips
Vegetable juice cocktail
Zucchini

The following raw vegetables may be used as desired:
Chicory
Chinese cabbage
Endive
Escarole
Lettuce
Parsley
Radishes
Watercress

Starchy vegetables are found in the bread exchange list.

Fruit Exchanges

(all fruits and fruit juices)

One exchange of fruit contains 10 grams of carbohydrate and 40 calories.

Apple	1 small
Apple juice	1/3 cup
Applesauce (unsweetened)	½ cup
Apricots, fresh	2 medium
Apricots, dried	4 halves
Banana	½ small
Berries	
Blackberries	½ cup
Blueberries	½ cup
Raspberries	½ cup
Strawberries	¾ cup
Cherries	10 large
Cider	1/3 cup
Dates	2
Figs, fresh	1
Figs, dried	1
Grapefruit	½
Grapefruit juice	½ cup
Grapes	12
Grape juice	¼ cup
Mango	½ small
Melon	
Cantaloupe	¼ small
Honeydew	⅛ medium
Watermelon	1 cup
Nectarine	1 small
Orange	1 small
Orange juice	½ cup
Papaya	¾ cup
Peach	1 medium
Pear	1 small
Persimmon, native	1 medium
Pineapple	½ cup
Pineapple juice	1/3 cup
Plums	2 medium
Prunes	2 medium
Prune juice	¼ cup
Raisins	2 tablespoons
Tangerine	1 medium

Cranberries may be used as desired if no sugar is added.

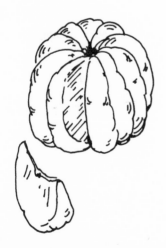

Tables

TABLE 1. Conversion Factors for Weights and Measures

To change	To	Multiply by
Inches	Centimeters	2.54
Meters	Inches	39.37
Fluid ounces	Cubic centimeters	29.57
Quarts	Liters	.946
Cubic centimeters	Fluid ounces	.034
Liters	Quarts	1.057
Ounces (av.)	Grams	28.35
Pounds (av.)	Kilograms	.454
Kilograms	Pounds	2.205
Kilocalories	KiloJoules	4.184

TABLE 2. Equivalent Weights and Measures

Volumes

	Metric	Household
1 fluid dram	4 millimeter	1 teaspoon (tsp)
1 fl oz	30 ml	2 tbsp (⅛ cup)
1½ fl oz	45 ml	1 jigger
2⅔ fl oz	80 ml	5⅓ tbsp (⅓ cup)
4 fl oz	118 ml	8 tbsp (½ cup)
8 fl oz	237 ml	1 cup
16 fl oz	473 ml	1 pint (pt)
32 fl oz	947 ml	1 quart (qt)
128 fl oz	3,785 ml	1 gallon (gal)

TABLE 3. Weights and Measures and Conversion Values

1 pound butter or margarine	= 4 sticks = 2 cups
	= 64 pats or squares
1 stick butter or margarine	= ½ cup
	= 16 pats or squares
1 tablespoon flour	= 1/4 ounce
1 cup flour	= 4-1/2 ounces
4 cups sifted all purpose flour	= 1 pound
4-1/2 cups sifted cake flour	= 1 pound
1 tablespoon sugar	= 3/5 ounce
1 cup sugar	= 10 ounces
2 cups granulated sugar	= 1 pound
2-2/3 cups confectioner's sugar	= 1 pound
2-2/3 cups brown sugar	= 1 pound
1 square of chocolate	= 1 ounce
1 ounce of chocolate	= 1/4 cup cocoa
8 average eggs	= 1 cup
8 to 10 egg whites	= 1 cup
12 to 14 egg yolks	= 1 cup
1 pound of walnuts or pecans in shell	= 1/2 pound shelled

TABLE 4. Herb Chart

	Basil	Bay	Marjoram	Oregano	Parsley	Peppermint
Appetizers	Tomato juice / Seafood cocktail	Tomato juice / Aspic		Tomato	Garnish	Fruit cup / Mellon balls / Cranberry juice
Soups	Tomato / Spinach	Stock / Herb bouquet	Spinach / Clam bouillon / Onion	Tomato / Bean	Any Garnish / Herb bouquet	Pea
Fish	Shrimp / Broiled fish / Fillets of fish / Mackerel	Bouillon	Broiled fish / Baked fish / Creamed fish	Stuffing	Any	
Eggs or Cheese	Scrambled eggs / Mock rarebit		Omelette aux fines herbes / Scrambled eggs	Boiled eggs	Creamed eggs / Scrambled eggs	
Meats	Liver / Lamb	Stews / Pot Roast / Shishkebob	Pot roast / Beef / Veal	Lamb / Meat loaf	Lamb / Veal / Steak / Stews	Lamb / Veal
Poultry and Game	Duck	Fricassee / Stews	Creamed chicken / Stuffings	Marinades / Stuffing	Stuffings / Herb bouquet	
Vegetables	Eggplant / Squash / Tomatoes / Onions	Boiled potatoes / Carrots / Stewed tomatoes	Carrots / Zucchini / Peas / Spinach	Tomatoes / Cabbage / Broccoli	Potatoes / Carrots / Peas	Carrots / New potatoes / Spinach / Zucchini
Salads	Tomato / Mixed green / Sea food	Fish salads / Aspic	Chicken / Mixed green	Tomato aspic / Fish salad	Potato / Fish / Mixed green	Fruit / Coleslaw / Orange / Pear
Sauces	Tomato / Spaghetti / Orange (for game) / Lemon (for fish)	All marinades	White sauce	Spaghetti / Tomato		Mint
Desserts and Beverages	Fruit compote	Custards				Fruit compote / Frostings / Ices / Tea

	Rosemary	Saffron	Sage	Savory	Tarragon	Thyme
Appetizers	Fruit cup		Cottage cheese / Cheese for spread	Vegetable juice cocktail	Fish cocktail / Tomato juice	Tomato juice / Fish cocktails
Soups	Pea / Spinach / Chicken	Fish consomme / Chicken	Cream soup / Chowders	Fish consomme / Bean	Consomme / Chicken / Tomato	Gumbo / Pea / Clam chowder / Vegetable
Fish	Salmon / Stuffings	Halibut	Stuffings	Broiled fish / Baked fish	Broiled fish / Mock lobster Newburg	Broiled fish / Baked fish
Eggs or Cheese	Scrambled eggs	Scrambled eggs	Cheddar spread / Cottage	Scrambled eggs / Deviled eggs	All egg dishes	Shirred eggs / Cottage cheese
Meats	Lamb / Veal ragout / Beef Stew	Veal	Stews	Veal	Veal	Meat loaf / Veal
Poultry and Game	Turkey / Chicken / Duck	Chicken	Turkey / Stuffings	Chicken / Stuffings	Chicken / Duck	Stuffings / Fricassee
Vegetables	Peas / Spinach / French-fried potatoes	Spanish rice / Rice	Lima beans / Eggplant / Onions / Tomatoes	Beans / Rice / Lentils / Sauerkraut	Salsify / Celery root / Mushrooms / Baked potatoes	Onions / Carrots / Beets
Salads	Fruit	Fish		Mixed green / String bean / Russian	Mixed green / Chicken / Fish	Pickled beets / Tomato / Aspics
Sauces	White sauce / Jelly	Fish sauce		Horseradish / Fish sauces	Bearn aise	Creole / Herb bouquets
Desserts and Beverages	Fruit compote	Cake / Frostings	Sage tea	Stewed pears		

Source: Adapted from the Spice Islands Herb Chart, and printed by permission of Spice Islands Company, South San Francisco, Calif.

References

ABRAM, H..S., ED. PSYCHOLOGICAL ASPECTS OF STRESS, SPRINGFIELD, ILLINOIS, CHARLES C. THOMAS, PUBLISHER, 1970.

ALVAREZ, W.C. (1943). NERVOUSNESS, INDIGESTION AND PAIN, NEW YORK: HOEBER.

AMERICAN HEART ASSOCIATION (1973). MONOGRAPH 38. IN CIRCULATION (MARCH, SUPPL. 1), 47.

AMERICAN MEDICAL ASSOCIATION, COUNCIL ON FOODS AND NUTRITION (1973 B.) F. AM. MED. ASSN. 225, 1118.

AMERICAN PSYCHIATRIC ASSOCIATION (1973). MEGAVITAMIN AND ORTHOMOLECULAR MEDICINE IN PSYCHIATRY. TASK FORCE REPORT NO. 87. WASHINGTON, D.C.

ANDERSON, G.H. (1977). IN ADVANCES IN NUTRITIONAL RESEARCH, ED. DRAPER, H.H., VOL. 1, P. 145. NEW YORK & LONDON: PLENUM PRESS.

ARCHER, J.E., AND BLACKMAN, D.E: 'PRENATAL PSYCHOLOGICAL STRESS AND OFFSPRING BEHAVIOR IN RATS AND MICE.' DEVELOP. PSYCHOBIOL. 4 (1971): 193-248.

ARENA, J.M. (1970). NUTRITION TODAY. P. 42.

AYDROYD, W.R. 7 DOUGHTY, J. (1970). WHEAT IN HUMAN NUTRITION. FAO NUTRITIONAL STUDIES, NO.23. ROME: FAO.

ASSOCIATION FOR RESEARCH IN NEVEROUS AND MENTAL DISEASE: LIFE STRESS AND BODILY DISEASES; PROCEEDINGS OF THE ASSOCIATION, DEC. 2 AND 3, 1949. EDITED BY H.G. WOLFF, S.G. WOLFF, JR., AND C.C. HARE. BALTIMORE.

BAIRD, J.D. (1973). IN SYMPOSIA: ANOREXIA NERVOSA, ED. BOERTSON, R.F. & PROUDFOOT, A.T., NO. 42, P. 83.

BARBORIAK, J.J. & MEADE, R.C. (1971). ATHEROSCLEROSIS L3, P. 199.

BARTLEY, S.H. , AND CHUTE, E. FATIGUE AND IMPAIRMENT IN MAN. FORWARD BY A.C. IVY, NEW YORK, LONDON: MCGRAW-HILL BOOK COMPANY, 1947.

BASOWITZ, H. PARSKY, H. HORCHIN, S.J. AND GRINKER, R.R. ANXIETY AND STRESS. NEW YORK, TORONTO, LONDON: MCGRAW-HILL CO., INC., 1954.

BING, R.J. & TILLMANNS, H. (1976). IN METABOLIC ASPECTS OF ALCOHOLISM, ED. LIEBER, C.S. P. 117. LANCASTER: MTP PRESS.

BIRCH, T.W. & GYORGY, P. (1936) BIOCHEM. F. 30, P. 304.

BLACK, D.A. K. (1968). ESSENTIALS OF FLUID BALANCE, 4TH. EDITION. OXFORD: BLACKWELL.

BLOOM, W.L. (1959). METABOLISM, 8, 214.

BOURNE, P.G. ED. THE PSYCHOLOGY AND PHYSIOLOGY OF STRESS. NEW YORK: ACADEMIC PRESS, INC., 1969.

BOVARD, E.W. "THE EFFECTS OF SOCIAL STIMULI ON THE RESPONSE TO STESS." PHYSIOL. REV. 66 (1959): 267-277.

BROWN, J. & 18 OTHERS (1970) WORLD REVIEW OF NUTRITION AND DIETETICS 12,34.

BRUCH, H. (1974) EATING DISORDERS, OBESITY, ANOREXIA NERVOSA AND THE PERSON WITHIN. LONDON: ROUTLEDGE AND KEGAN PAUL.

BUTTERWORTH, C.E., JR.,BAUGH, C.M., AND KRUMDIECK, C. (1966). J. CLIM. INVEST. 48, 1131.

CAHILL, G.F. (1975). IN OBESITY IN PERSPECTIVE. ED. BRAY, G.A. DHEW PUBLICATION NO. (NIH) 75-708, P. 58. WASHINGTON,D.C. SUPERINTENDENT OF DOCUMENTS.

CANNON, W.B. BODILY CHANGES IN PAIN, HUNGER, FEAR, AND RAGE. BOSTON: CHARLES T. BRANFORD COMPNAY, 1953.

CARLSON, L.A. (ED.).(1972). NUTRITION IN OLD AGE. SYMPOSIA OF THE SWEDISH NUTRITION X UPPSALA: ALMOVIST & WICKSELL.

CARLSON, L.A., OLSSON, A.G., ORO, L. AND ROSSNER, S. (1971). ARTHEROSCLEROSIS 14, 391.

CHAN, P. C. & COHEN, L.A. (1975). CANCER RESEARCH. 35. 3384.

CLEMENTS, F.W. & WISHART, J.W. (1956). METABOLISM 5, 623.

COOK, G.C. (1973). IN INTESTINAL ENZYME DEFICIENCIES, ED. BORGSTROM, B. DAHLOUIST,A. AND HAMBREUS, L. UPPSALA: ALMOVIST AND WICKSELL.

COOK, P. (1971). BR. F. CANCER, 25. 853.

CRAIG, I.H., BELL, F.P. , GOLDSMITH, CH.H. AND SCHWARTZ, C.J. (1973). ARTHEROSCLEROSIS 18, 277.

DARKE, S.J. & STEPHEN, J.ML. (1976). VITAMIN D DEFICIENCY AND OSTEOMALACIA. LONDON: HMSO.

DE WYS, W. (1970). CANCER RESEARCH. 30 28L6.

DUNBAR, F. EMOTIONS AND BODILY CHANGES. NEW YORK; COLUMBIA UNIVERSITY PRESS, 1947. SURVEY OF THE LITERATURE BETWEEN 1910 AND 1945 ON PSYCHO-SOMATIC INTERRELATIONS

DUNN, W.L., JR., ED. SMOKING BEHAVIOR: MOTIVES AND INCENTIVES. INTRODUCTION BY HANS SELYE. NEW YORK: JOHN WILEY AND SONS, 1973.

ENGLE, E.T. AND PINCUS, G. EDITORS. HORMONES AND THE AGING PROCESS. NEW YORK: ACADEMIC PRESS, INC., 1956.

FARBER, S.M.: MUSTRAACHI AND WILSON, R.H.L., EDITORS. MAN UNDER STRESS. BEREKELY, LOS ANGELES: UNIVERSITY OF CALIFORNIA PRESS, 1964.

FOURMAN, P. & ROYER, P. (1968). CALCIUM METABOLISM AND THE BONE. OXFORD: BLACKWELL.

FUNKENSTEIN, D.H., KING,S.H. AND DROLETTE, M.E. MASTERY OF STRESS. CAMBRIDGE: HARVARD UNIVERSITY PRESS, 1957.

GIERSTEN, J.C. "SUDDEN DEATH FROM NATURAL CAUSES.± ARB UNIVERSITY. BERGEN MEDICAL SERVICES. NO. 1 (1962), 1-52.

GRINKER, R.R. AND SPIEGEL, J.P. MEN UNDER STESS. PHILADELPHIA: THE BLACKISTON COMPANY, 1945.

GROSS, N.E. LIVING WITH STRESS. FORWARD BY HAN SELYE. NEW YORK, TORONTO, LONDON: MCGRAW-HILL BOOK COMPANY, INC. 1958.

HEATON, K.W. (1973). PLANT FOODS FOR MAN. L,33.

HODGE, H.C. (1964). IN MINERAL METABOLISM. VOL. 2, PART A. ED. COMAR, CL.L. AND BRONNER, F.P. 573, NEW YORK: ACADEMIC PRESS.

JANIS, I.L. PSYCHOLOGICAL STRESS. NEW YORK: JOHN WILEY AND SONS, INC. 1958.

KERNER, F. STRESS AND YOUR HEART. INTRODUCTION BY HANS SELYE. NEW YORK: HAWTHORNE BOOKS, INC., 1961.

KOLLAR, E.J. "PSYCHOLOGICAL STRESS: A RE-EVALUATION." JOURNAL OF NERVOUS AND MENTAL DISEASES. 132 (1961): 832-896.

KOSITSKIY, G.L. AND SMIRNOV, V.S. THE NERVOUS SYSTEM AND STRESS. WASHINGTON,D.C., NATIONAL AERONAUTICS AND SPACE ADMINISTRATION, 1972.

KRAUS, H. BACKACHE, STRESS, AND TENSION: THEIR CAUSE, PREVENTION, AND TREATMENT. NEW YORK: SIMON AND SCHUSTER, INC., 1962.

KREHL, W.A. (1973). IN MODERN NUTRITION IN HEALTH AND DISEASE. 5TH. EDITION. GOODHART, R.S. AND SHILS, M.E.. PHILADELPHIA: LEA AND FEBIGER.

LABORIT, H. ORGANIC REACTION TO STRESS AND SHOCK (REACTION ORGANIQUE A L'AGRESSION ET. CHOC). PREFACE BY R. LERICHE. PARIS: MASSON AND CIE, EDITEURS, 1952.

LASS, D.C. AND SINGER, J.E. URBAN STRESS: EXPERIMENTS ON NOISE AND SOCIAL STRESSORS. NEW YORK, LONDON: ACADEMIC PRESS, INC., 1972.

LEVINE, S. "STRESS AND BEHAVIOR". SCIENTIFIC AMERICAN, 224 (1971): P. 16-3L.

LLOYD-STILL,J.D. (1976). MALNUTRITION AND INTELLECTUAL DEVELOPMENT. LANCASTER MTP.

MASLOW, A.H. MOTIVATION AND PERSONALITY. NEW YORK: HARPER BROTHERS, INC. 1954.

MCKENNA, M. REVITALIZE YOURSELF: THE TECHNIQUE OF STAYING YOUTHFUL. FORWARD BY J.A. BAILEY, NEW YORK: HAWTHORNE BOOKS, INC., 1972.

MAYMAN, M. AND PRUYSER, P. THE VITAL BALANCE: THE LIFE PROCESS IN MENTAL HEALTH AND ILLNESS. NEW YORK: THE VIKING PRESS, INC.1863.

MITCHELL, H.G. AND EDMAN, M. NUTRITION AND CLIMATIC STRESS. SPRINGFIELD, ILLINOIS: CHARLES C. THOMAS, PUBLISHER. 1951.

OGRYZLO, M.A. (1965) ARTHRITIS RHEUMATISM. 8, P. 799.

ROSS, M.H. (1976). IN NUTRITION AND AGING, ED. WINICK, M. NEW YORK: WILEY PUBLISHING COMPANY.

SMITH, E.B. AND SLATER, R. (1970) ARHEROSCLEROSIS, VOL. II, P. 4L7.

SORENSON, S. THE QUEST OF WHOLENESS. REYKJAVIL: PRENSTMIDJUA JONS HELGASONAR. 1971.

TOFFLER, A. FUTURE SHOCK. NEW YORK: RANDOM HOUSE, INC., 1970.

WARMBRAND, M. ADD YEARS TO YOUR LIFE. NEW YORK: WHITTIER BOOKS, INC. 1954.

WIGGERS, C.J. PHYSIOLOGY OF SHOCK. LONDON: OXFORD UNIVERSITY PRESS, 1950.

WOLFF, H.G. STRESS AND DISEASE. SPRINGFIELD, ILLINOIS: CHARLES C. THOMAS PUBLISHER, 1953.

Stress Questionnaire
to Dietitians and Nutritionists

1. Do you find the people you serve, patients, students and others living under excess stress? yes no

2. Are the audiences that you address in diet counseling willing to express basic causes of stresses, physical, mental, psychological or emotional? yes no

3. Are you aware of personal stresses, career or otherwise? yes no

4. Do your Nutrition Assessment Studies include the client stresses which relate to changes in food patterns? yes no

5. Do your eating patterns change when you experience stress? yes no

6. What food, food patterns or lifestyle are you promoting in your teaching or counseling sessions?

7. When you arrive home after work what food do you eat or drink first?

8. What foods or beverages do you recommend for stress?

9. How do you relieve your stresses?

10. What groups of foods do you feel more nearly relate to stress relief? Soups Beverages Main dishes Breads Vegetables Salads Desserts

Note: Please include 1 or 2 recipes for each group checked

11. Check patient diseases you feel more nearly relate to

   heart disease Kidney disease Circulatory disease

   Hypertension Diabetes Eye disease

   Liver disease All above equally related

12. List the foods in the following groups that you feel will most likely relieve stress:

   a. Soups

   b. Beverages

   c. Main dishes

   d. Breads

   e. Vegetables

   f. Salads

   g. Desserts

Note: Please send recipes that you would like to share

   In summary, list your recommendations for preventing stresses in daily life.

Index